Thomas O'Conor

Rubber hand stamps and the manipulation of rubber

A practical treatise on the manufacture of India rubber hand stamps

Thomas O´Conor

Rubber hand stamps and the manipulation of rubber
A practical treatise on the manufacture of India rubber hand stamps

ISBN/EAN: 9783337224479

Printed in Europe, USA, Canada, Australia, Japan

Cover: Foto ©Lupo / pixelio.de

More available books at **www.hansebooks.com**

Rubber Hand Stamps

* * * *

AND THE

Manipulation of Rubber

A PRACTICAL TREATISE ON THE MANUFACTURE OF INDIA RUBBER HAND STAMPS, SMALL ARTICLES OF INDIA RUBBER, THE HEKTOGRAPH, SPECIAL INKS, CEMENTS, AND ALLIED SUBJECTS

BY

T. O'CONOR SLOANE, A.M., E.M., Ph.D.

Author of
"Home Experiments in Science," "Arithmetic of Electricity," etc.

FULLY ILLUSTRATED

NEW YORK
NORMAN W. HENLEY & CO.
150 NASSAU STREET
1891

COPYRIGHT, 1890, BY
NORMAN W. HENLEY & CO.

PREFACE.

The present work hardly needs a preface. The object is to present in the simplest form the subject of the manipulation of india rubber. To mould and cure the mixed gum but few appliances are needed, and these can be made at home. The articles produced are of more than ordinary utility. These two facts give value to the art and furnish a *raison d'être* for this book. If its instructions do not prove practical it will have missed its object.

For some reason the methods of moulding the material are not generally known. Experiment has taught many the futility of attempting to melt and cast it. While thus intractable by the usual methods, it is the most plastic of materials when properly treated. Its power of reproducing the finest details of a mould, of entering all the intricacies and undercuttings of a design, cause one to feel a peculiar pleasure in working with so responsive a material. It is not saying too much to affirm that to some readers this book will disclose a long hidden secret. To make it more generally useful it is written for such readers, to meet the want of those knowing of the subject. It was felt that in following this course, and in treating the subject from its first steps, including the simplest as well as most advanced methods, the book would appeal to a larger body of readers.

The allied subjects to which some chapters are devoted will be acceptable to many readers. The hektograph is given in several modifications. A substitute for rubber stamps which stands the severe usage of the Post Office has very distinct merits, and the manufacture is accordingly described in detail. Cements and inks embody many special formulæ. In the last chapter interesting and practical notes will be found.

For the use of certain cuts we are under obligations to the Buffalo Dental Manufacturing Co., Messrs. E. & F. N. Spon & Co., and to Mr. L. Spangenberg.

CONTENTS.

CHAPTER I.

THE SOURCES OF INDIA RUBBER AND ITS HISTORY.

The Trees—The Sap—Caoutchouc—Early Uses by the Indians—First knowledge of it in Europe—Goodyear, Day, and Mackintosh............................ 9

CHAPTER II.

THE NATURAL HISTORY AND COLLECTION OF INDIA RUBBER.

African, East Indian, Central and South American Gums—Different Methods of Collection and Coagulation... 15

CHAPTER III.

PROPERTIES OF UNVULCANIZED AND VULCANIZED INDIA RUBBER.

Properties of Unvulcanized Rubber; its Cohesion and importance of this property—Analysis of Sap and Caoutchouc—Effects of Heat and Cold—Distillation Products—Vulcanized Rubber, and its Properties...... 24

CHAPTER IV.

THE MANUFACTURE OF MASTICATED, MIXED SHEET AND VULCANIZED INDIA RUBBER.

Treatment by the Manufacturer—Washing and Sheet-

vi   CONTENTS.

ing—Masticating—Making Sheeting and Threads—Mixing—Curing—Coated Tissues.......................... 35

CHAPTER V.

INDIA RUBBER STAMP MAKING.

Mixed Sheet—Outlines of Moulding—Home-Made Vulcanizing Press—Further Simplifications of Same—Securing Accurate Parallelism of Platen and Bed—Distance Pieces—Wood vs. Iron as Material for Press—Use of Springs on the Home-Made Press—Metal Flask Clamps—Large Gas-Heated Vulcanizing Press—Preparing Type Model—The Matrix—Plaster of Paris and Dental Plaster as Substances for Matrices—Dextrine and Gum Arabic Solutions for Mixing Matrix—How Matrix is made—Shellac Solution for Matrix—Matrix Press and Spring-Chase—How to retard the Setting of Plaster of Paris—Oxychloride of Zinc Matrices—Talc Powder—Moulding and Curing the Stamp—Kerosene Heating Stove—Manipulation of Press—Degree of Heat—Simple Test of Curing—Time Required—Combined Matrix Making and Vulcanizing Apparatus—Chamber Vulcanizers—Object of Steam in Vulcanizers—Temperature Corresponding to Different Steam Pressures—Jacketed Vulcanizers—Gas Regulator—Flower Pot Vulcanizer—Fish Kettle Vulcanizer—Making Stamps without any Apparatus Whatever—Notes on Type, Quadrats and Spaces—Autograph Stamps.............. 47

CHAPTER VI.

INDIA RUBBER TYPE MAKING.

Movable Type Making—Simple Flask and Matrix—Precautions as to Quantity of Rubber—Moulding—Curing—Cutting Type Apart—Special Steel Moulds—Wooden Bodied Type.............................. 73

CONTENTS.

CHAPTER VII.
THE MAKING OF STAMPS AND TYPE FROM VULCANIZED INDIA RUBBER.

Ready Vulcanized Gum as Material for Stamps—Simplicity of the Process of Using It—Advantages and Disadvantages—Availability for Type............ 77

CHAPTER VIII.
VARIOUS TYPE MATRICES FOR RUBBER STAMPS AND TYPES.

Electrotype Matrices—Papier Maché—Flong Paste—Flong Matrices—Beating into Model—Drying and Baking—Struck-up Matrices—Chalk Plates............... 80

CHAPTER IX.
THE MAKING OF VARIOUS SMALL ARTICLES OF INDIA RUBBER.

Suction Discs—Pencil Tips—Cane and Chair Leg Tips—Corks—Mats—Cord and Tubes—Bulbs and Hollow Toys.. 85

CHAPTER X.
THE MANIPULATION OF SHEET RUBBER GOODS.

Sheet Rubber Articles—Toy Balloons—Uses of Sheet Rubber in the Laboratory............................. 94

CHAPTER XI.
VARIOUS VULCANIZING AND CURING PROCESSES.

Liquid Curing Baths—Sulphur Bath—Haloids and Nitric Acid as Vulcanizers—Alkaline Sulphides—Sulphur Absorption Process—Parke's Process............ 97

CHAPTER XII.
THE SOLUTION OF INDIA RUBBER.

Mastication with Solvent—Peculiarities of the Pro-

viii   *CONTENTS.*

cess—Different Solvents and their Properties—Paraffin—Vulcanized Rubber Solution—Aqueous Solution..... 103

CHAPTER XIII.
EBONITE, VULCANITE AND GUTTA-PERCHA.

Ebonite and Vulcanite—Manufacture—Manipulation—Gutta-Percha and its Manipulation 108

CHAPTER XIV.
GLUE OR COMPOSITION STAMPS.

Substitute for Rubber Stamps—The United States Government Formula—Models and Moulds—Dating—Handles.. 113

CHAPTER XV.
THE HEKTOGRAPH.

How Made—The French Government Formula—Hektograph Sheets.................................... 121

CHAPTER XVI.
CEMENTS.

Marine Glue, and other special Cements............. 125

CHAPTER XVII.
INKS.

Hektograph, Stencil and Marking Inks—White and Metallic Inks.. 129

CHAPTER XVIII.
MISCELLANEOUS.

Preservation and Renovation of India Rubber—Burned Rubber for Artists—India Rubber Substitutes—General Notes of Interest......................... 134

RUBBER HAND STAMP MAKING AND THE MANIPULATION OF RUBBER.

CHAPTER I.

THE SOURCES OF INDIA RUBBER AND ITS HISTORY.

India rubber or caoutchouc is a very peculiar product, which is found in and extracted from the juice of certain trees and shrubs. These are quite numerous and are referred for the most part to the following families: Euphorbiaceæd, Urticaceæd, Artocarpeæd, Asclepiadaceæd, and Cinchonaceæd. It is evident that a considerable number of trees are utilized in commerce for its production, and it is certain that it exists, quite widely distributed, in many cases as a constituent of the juice of plants not recognized as containing it.

When an india rubber tree is tapped, which is effected by making incisions in the bark, the sap of the tree exudes. It is a milky substance and is collected in various ways; it may be in vessels of clay, in shells, or in other receptacles by the india rubber hunters. If this substance is examined it is found to be of very remarkable and characteristic constitution, resembling in its physical features ordinary milk. It is composed of from fifty to ninety per cent. of water, in which is suspended in microscopic globules, like the cream in milk, the desired caoutchouc or india rubber. If the juice is left to stand in vessels, like milk in a creamery, the globules rise to the surface, and a cream of india rubber can be skimmed off from the surface. If the juice is evaporated over a fire, the water escapes and the india rubber remains. By dipping an article repeatedly in the juice and drying it, a thick or thin coating of india rubber can be developed. Before the modern methods for the manipulation of the gum had been developed, and before the invention of vulcanization, this method was adopted for the manufacture of shoes. The original "india rubbers" for protection of the feet in wet weather were made in this manner. A clay last was used, upon which the india rubber was deposited as described. The clay last was then broken out and removed. Great quantities of overshoes were thus made in South America, and many were exported to Europe.

When caoutchouc has once been removed from this watery emulsion, which for all practical purposes is a solution, it cannot be restored to the former state of liquidity; it remains solid. It will absorb a considerable quantity of water, but will not enter again into the *quasi* solution or combination. This property of permanent coagulation, which interferes to a degree with its easy manipulation, was early discovered. In the last century quantities of the natural milk were exported to Europe to be used in what may be termed the natural process of manufacture, because once solidified it could not be redissolved, and because the manufacturers of those days had not the present methods of dealing with the apparently intractable gum.

The natives of South America before the advent of Europeans, were familiar with the treatment of the juice by evaporation just described and used to make bottles, shoes and syringes of it for their own use. The name *Siphonia* applied to several species of rubber tree, and *seringa* (caoutchouc) and *seringari* (caoutchouc gatherer) in Spanish recall the old Indian syringes and tubes.

The gum is now collected for export in many parts of the world. South and Central America are, as they have always been, the greatest producers. Some is collected in Africa, Java and India. The best comes from Para. However carefully treated a great difference is found in the product from different countries. The Brazilian india rubber, known as Para, from the port of shipment, ranks as the best in the market.

Its history as far as recorded, does not go back of the last century. Le Condamine, who explored the

Amazon River, sent from South America in 1736 to the *Institute de France,* in Paris, the first sample of india rubber ever seen in Europe. He accompanied the sample with a communication. He said that the Indians of that country used the gum in making several domestic objects of utility, such as vessels, bottles, boots, waterproof clothing, etc. He stated that it was attacked and to a certain extent dissolved by warm nut oil. In 1751 and 1768 other samples were received through MM. Fresnau and Macquer, who sent them to the Academy of Sciences, Paris, from Cayenne in Guiana.

Although from this period numerous experiments were tried with the new substance little of importance was done with it for many years. Its first use was to rub out pencil marks, whence it derived its name of "india rubber." As late as 1820 this continued to be its principal use.

An interesting reminiscence of its early history is given by Joseph Priestley, the great English chemist of the last century, celebrated as the discoverer of oxygen. In 1770 he mentioned the use of the gum for erasing pencil marks, and speaks of its cost being three shillings, about seventy cents, for "a cubical piece of about half an inch."

As we have seen, its solubility was early studied. In 1761 Hérissant added turpentine, ether and "huile de Dippel" to the list of solvents. In 1793 its solubility was utilized in France by Besson, who made waterproof cloth. In 1797 Johnson introduced for the same manufacture a solution in mixed turpentine and alcohol.

The year 1820 is the beginning of the period of its modern use on a more extended scale. Nadier developed the methods of cutting it into sheets and threads and of weaving the latter. Mackintosh in 1823 began the manufacture of waterproof cloth, using the solution of the gum in coal tar naptha, which was caused to deposit by evaporation a layer of the gum upon a piece of cloth which was covered by a second one. This protected the wearer from the gummy and sticky coating of raw india rubber. At the best the original Mackintoshes must have been very disagreeable articles for wear.

In 1825 india rubber shoes of raw india rubber were imported from South America and formed for a while an important article of commerce.

In 1839 Charles Goodyear, of Massachusetts, invented the art of vulcanizing, or combining india rubber with sulphur. It was patented on June 15, 1844, and covers only the manufacture of soft rubber. Vulcanite or hard rubber (whalebone rubber) is disputed as to its origin, its invention being assigned by some to Nelson Goodyear and by others to Austin G. Day, of Connecticut. Goodyear however succeeded in obtaining a patent on May 6, 1851. Day obtained a patent on August 10, 1858.

Vulcanization is the most important invention ever made in connection with india rubber and may fairly rank as one of the greatest discoveries of the present century. It is claimed by the English, an inventor named Handcock being cited as the rival of Charles Goodyear. The latter inventor had as an associate Nathaniel Hayward, who is probably entitled to some of the credit.

By vulcanization india rubber loses susceptibility to heat and cold, becomes non-adherent, and insoluble in almost all substances. It is converted from a comparatively useless substance into one of wide applicability.

The subject of india rubber is so interesting in its theoretical as well as practical bearings that it seems impossible that those who are workers in it should not feel an interest in its natural history. For such readers the chapter on the natural history and collection of india rubber has been written. As it is a product of widely separated lands on both hemispheres, and as it is yielded by an immense number of plants, it is impossible in the limits of a chapter to give a full outline of its natural history.

The chapter in question is, therefore, with this apology, inserted where it belongs, near the beginning of the book. Those who are entirely practical may pass it over. There is no doubt that the few minutes necessary for its perusal will be bestowed upon it by some.

CHAPTER II.

THE NATURAL HISTORY AND COLLECTION OF INDIA RUBBER.

African india rubber is mostly exported from the west coast. The belt of country producing it extends nearly across the continent. Those who are familiar with the india rubber plants of our conservatories are apt to think of the gum as the product of trees, but in Africa it is largely yielded by climbing plants of very numerous varieties, belonging generally to the Landolphia species. It is collected by the natives by careless or desultory methods, probably less advanced than the ways followed by the South Americans. Possibly its marked inferiority may be partly attributed to this. It is also supposed by many that, were the gathering restricted to the vine producing the best gum, better results would follow. As it is now all gums are mixed indiscriminately. African gum is of very inferior quality.

The African india rubber vines grow often in dark moist ravines, where no valuable product other than themselves could be cultivated. They are entirely wild. The vines when cut exude an abundance of sap, which differs from the South American product in its quickness of coagulation. As it escapes from the wound it at once solidifies and prevents the further escape of juice. The negroes are said to employ the following highly original method of collecting it. They make long gashes in the bark. As fast as the milky juice comes out they wipe it off with their fingers and wipe these in turn on their arms, shoulders, and body. In this way they form a thick covering of inspissated juice or caoutchouc over the upper part of their body. This from time to time is removed by peeling. It is then said to be cut up and boiled in water. This is one account. According to others the natives remove a large piece of bark, so that the juice runs out and is collected in holes in the earth or on leaves. Wooden vessels are said to be used elsewhere. Sometimes the juice is said to be collected upon the arms, the dried caoutchouc coming off in the shape of tubes. A clew to the inferiority of African india rubber is afforded by the statement that too deep a cut liberates a gum which deteriorates the regular product if it mixes with it. The drying of the gum is thought to have much to do with its quality and it is highly probable that this affects the African product. Some samples seem to be partly decomposed they are so highly offensive in odor. The South American rubber is often dried in thin layers, one over the other, by a smoky fire, which may have an antiseptic effect upon the newly coagulated caoutchouc. No such process as far as known is used in Africa.

The African india rubber appears under different names in commerce. From the Congo region lumps of no particular shape called "knuckles"; from Sierra Leone smooth lumps, "negro-heads," and "balls" made up of small scrap; from the Portuguese ports "thimbles," "nuts," and "negro-heads;" from the gaboon "tongues;" and from Liberia "balls are received." It is all characterized by great adhesiveness and low elasticity.

From Assam, Java, Penang, and Rangoon there is considerable gum exported. It is supposed to be the product of trees of the *ficus* species, in all these places, as it is known to be in Java and Assam. In the latter place rigid restrictions are imposed as far as possible upon the gathering. In the case of wild trees scattered through the forest the carrying out of these restrictions is not practicable. The trees are cut with knives in long incisions through the bark and the juice is collected in holes dug in the ground, or often in leaves wrapped up into a conical form, somewhat as grocers form their wrapping paper into cornucopia shape for holding sugar, etc.

It has seemed reasonably certain that the india rubber producing plants might be cultivated with profit, and it is as certainly to be feared that without such cultivation they will become extinct. Efforts have been made in the direction of raising them artificially but without much success. In Assam numerous experiments have been made to propagate the india rubber bearing *ficus* tree.

A good instance of the ill effects of carelessness in the original gathering of the crop is afforded by the Bornese collectors. The source of Borneo india rubber is a variety of creepers. These are cut down and divided into short sections from a few inches to a yard in length. The sap oozes out from the ends. To accelerate its escape the pieces are sometimes heated at one end. It is coagulated by salt water. Sometimes a salt called *nipa* salt, obtained by burning a certain plant (*nipa fruticans*), is used for the purpose. In either case it is coagulated

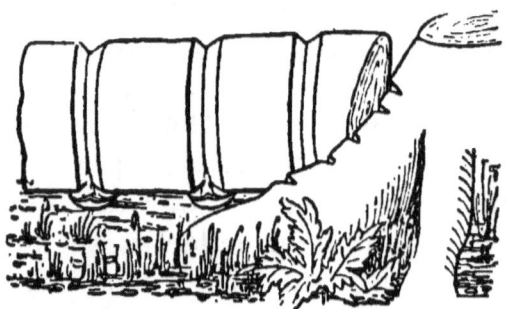

TREE FELLED FOR COLLECTION OF INDIA RUBBER.

into rough balls and masses. These masses are heavily charged with the salt water, often containing as much as fifty per cent., and rarely much less than twenty per cent.

Central America and Panama are great producers of the gum. In Panama the custom of felling the trees is often adopted. In this case grooves are cut around the prostrate trunk, and under each groove as the trunk lies on the ground a vessel is placed to collect the sap. Its coagulation is often effected by leaving it for a couple of weeks standing at rest in a hole, excavated on the surface of the ground, and covered over with leaves. The caoutchouc separates under these conditions. A quicker method, but one yielding an inferior product, is obtained by adding to the fresh juice some bruised leaves of a plant (*ipomœa bona nox*) which acts something like acid upon milk, in separating the desired solid matter or caoutchouc. A jelly like accretion saturated with blackish water is thus obtained. By working it together a blackish liquid is caused to escape, and comparatively pure gum is gradually obtained. As much as one hundred pounds of india rubber may be obtained from a single tree where this destructive system is employed. Further north, where a better counsel has prevailed, the trees are only tapped, and the india rubber hunter is satisfied if from a tree eighteen inches in diameter he obtains twenty gallons of sap, giving fifty pounds of gum. Even where tapping is done the tree is often destroyed by carelessness or ignorance.

Two systems are followed in Nicaragua. The operator ascends by a ladder if he has one, or in any case climbs as high as he well can and begins to make a long incision. Sometimes he carries one long straight cut clear down to the ground. This is made the starting point for a number of side cuts, short, and running diagonally into it. This is also one of the Brazilian methods. The Nicaraguan sometimes also makes two spiral incisions, one right-handed and the other left-handed, crossing each other as they descend so as to divide the surface of the tree into roughly outlined diamonds. In either case the juice flows down to an iron spout, placed at the bottom of the tree, which spout leads to an iron pail. The milk is gathered and passed through a sieve, and coagulated in barrels by the *ipomœa* plant as before mentioned. This gives three grades of rubber. The bulk is obtained from the barrels and is called often *méros;* the small lump which forms in the spout is rolled into a ball and called *cabezza;* the dried strips pulled out of the cuts is of very good quality and is called *bola* or *burucha.*

From Brazil is exported the famous Para india rubber. This is of very high quality, and is greatly esteemed by all manufacturers. No process can make a poor gum give a really good product. The system of gathering it varies. Sometimes the tree is cut into by gashes from an axe, such gashes extending in a row all around the trunk. Under each gash a small clay cup is luted fast with some fresh mixed clay. These collect from a tablespoonful of juice upward, which is collected, and the cups are removed on the same day. The next day a second row of cuts is made below the others, and the same process is repeated. This is continued until from a point as high as a man can reach, down to the ground the tree is full of cuts. Sometimes a gutter of clay is found partly around the trunk with gashes above it. In other cases a vine is secured

TREE TAPPED FOR INDIA RUBBER.

around the tree and a collecting gutter is worked with it for a basis.

The juice is coagulated in a smoky fire. A bottomless jar is placed over the fire and some palm nuts are mixed with the fuel. The mould, which is often a canoe paddle, is smeared with clay to prevent adhesion and is then heated. A cup of juice is poured over it, and after the excess has dropped off it is moved about rapidly over the smoke and hot air which ascends from the mouth of the jar. This series of operations is repeated until the coating is quite thick; it may be as much as five inches. After solidifying over night it is cut open and the paddle or mould is removed. After a few days dry-

INDIAN DRYING AND SMOKING INDIA RUBBER.

ing it is sent to market. With all the heating, during which it sweats profusely, it still retains fifteen per cent. of water.

India rubber sap may be coagulated by an aqueous solution of alum. The process has been tried in Brazil, and is used to a considerable extent in

Pernambuco. It was proposed by an investigator named *Strauss*, and the process is still called by his name. One objection is that it gives a very wet product, and apparently one of inferior value to the smoked gum.

The feeling that india rubber suffers in the gathering has been so much felt that it has been recently suggested that if possible the uncoagulated juice should be exported to Europe there to be worked up from the beginning.

CHAPTER III.

PROPERTIES OF UNVULCANIZED AND VULCANIZED INDIA RUBBER.

There are two broad divisions to which all varieties of india rubber can be assigned—unvulcanized and vulcanized rubber. Speaking with a certain amount of license it may be said that more properties characterize the former than the latter. The vulcanized article is very slightly affected by ordinary changes of temperature, cannot to any considerable extent be changed by heat short of absolute destruction or decomposition, cannot be united or moulded except in simple forms, is highly elastic, and is insoluble in almost every solvent for ordinary caoutchouc.

Unvulcanized caoutchouc possesses very interesting and peculiar properties. The first part of the present chapter is devoted to this substance. Those who have never seen the crude gum as imported are familiar with the article almost pure in the form of sheet rubber and black rubber articles generally. These are of nearly pure caoutchouc, though recently the tendency is to vulcanize them to a considerable degree.

A piece of pure gum containing no combined sulphur, iodine, or other vulcanizing constituent will be found to exhibit a very striking peculiarity. Two freshly cut surfaces when placed in contact will adhere. This is not in consequence of any viscous or sticky coating. When india rubber is cut the surface is perfectly dry and non-adherent except to itself.

The writer once had this property of adhesion brought strongly to his attention. In some analytical investigations of coal gas he had proposed to use finely divided india rubber as an absorbent of sulphur. This constituent it absorbs from gas, and it seemed that a basis for a quantitative determination of sulphur might be found in such property. Accordingly some raw india rubber was procured and with some trouble was cut up into little pieces which were put into a bottle. A day or two afterwards the pieces united wherever they were in contact, and an irregular cavernous lump was the result. This involved no melting or softening or change of shape. Each little piece was there intact and distinct but firmly attached to its neighbors.

The analogy of this action is seen in lead. Two fresh surfaces brought together, preferably with a twisting or wrenching pressure, adhere quite firmly. The adherence of india rubber and of lead each to itself is often exhibited by physical lecturers as an illustration of cohesion. The cohesion of india rubber is however far more perfect than that of lead, probably because of its comparatively great resistance to oxidation, and because, owing to its elasticity larger areas can be brought in contact. Comparatively great though this resistance to oxidation is, oxygen, especially in the allotropic modification known as ozone, may act quite powerfully on the gum. Sunlight also can affect it injuriously.

A more familiar illustration of the uniting of two pieces of the same material is seen in the welding of iron. The blacksmith heats two pieces of iron until they are nearly white hot and are pasty in consistency. On placing them in contact and hammering to force them together they unite so firmly as to be practically one. It is necessary that the surfaces of clean metal should be brought together. If the pressure induced by the hammering is insufficient to bring this about, a flux is added which dissolves the oxide and causes the metal to come in contact with metal and to weld. The analogy with india rubber in its cohesive action is evident. Surfaces long exposed or which are dusty do not cohere. The relegation of ice is similar in effect.

The cohesion of india rubber is important and should be thoroughly appreciated. It is not saying too much to assert that the entire treatment of the raw gum depends upon this interesting property. The great lumps of gum are torn to pieces and washed free from gravel and dirt without going to powder, because owing to their elasticity they yield and as fast as torn apart the pieces tend to reunite. Again india rubber is mixed with pigments and vulcanizing reagents by a method practically one of grinding or masticating, but the material while it changes its shape, and by the admixture of the various ingredients becomes less strong or easier torn, still remains intact, as it welds together or coheres as fast as disintegrated.

As regards its chemical constitution the sap of a Para rubber tree has been analyzed with the following general results: (Faraday).

Caoutchouc	80.70
Albuminous, extractive, and saline matter, etc	12.93
Water	56.37
	100.00

Its specific gravity is 1.012.

Caoutchouc itself or raw india rubber is a mixture of several hydrocarbons of the following composition in general:

Carbon	87.5
Hydrogen	12.5
	100.0

Its specific gravity is from .912 to .942.

The hydrocarbons composing it are isomeric or polymeric with turpentine. This fact brings it well within the range of familiar vegetable products. As will be seen the products of its distillation fall among the same polymers and isomers.

When pure it is nearly colorless, the dark color being due to impurities. In thin sheets it is almost or quite transparent. It burns readily, and with a very luminous, smoky flame, as might have been anticipated from its composition. The action of heat and cold on it is dependent on the degree of the temperature. At ordinary temperature it is elastic and firm. It can be stretched and will return almost to its original size when released from tension. Yet the return to its shape is so liable to be incomplete, especially after long sustained stretching, that pure unvulcanized india rubber is considered imperfectly elastic.

Any elasticity it possesses is principally elasticity of shape as distinguished from elasticity of volume. In other words when pressed or stretched it may change shape to a great extent but hardly change its volume at all. A cube of $2\frac{1}{2}$ inches under a weight of 200 tons lost 1-10 of its volume only. This is largely due to the fact that it represents an approximately solid body, or one destitute of considerable physical pores. Solids and liquids are very slightly compressible. Whatever degree of compressibility caoutchouc possesses is due principally to its minute pores.

If the temperature is reduced to the freezing point of water a piece of raw india rubber becomes rigid and stiff. On application of heat it returns to its former pliable condition. The same return to flexibility may be brought about by stretching it mechanically. This may be rather a fallacy. Stretching india rubber warms it, so that in this mechanically imparted rise of temperature we may find at least a probable cause of the softening.

If the temperature is raised several effects are produced, according to circumstances. A piece which has been stretched and held stretched, has its tension increased by a degree of heat considerably less than that of boiling water. Some offer the theory that it contains air enclosed in its pores which, expanding, produces this effect. As the boiling point is reached the material softens and becomes somewhat plastic, so that it can be moulded into shape to a considerable extent and stretched to threads of great fineness. Its elasticity also disappears as the heat is maintained. These effects increase in extent up to a heat of 248° F. (120° C.). The return to its original state is not immediate however. Some time is required before the reduction of temperature will have full effect.

If now a still higher degree of heat is applied, 392° F. (200° C.) the india rubber softens to a viscous body, or melts. From this state it cannot be restored. It remains permanently "burned" or melted whatever is done to it. Some attempt at hardening may be made by the use of vulcanizing chemicals, but the result will be very imperfect.

A further increase of heat brings about a destructive distillation. India rubber treated in a retort to a heat exceeding 400° F. (204° C.) evolves volatile hydrocarbons of oily consistency, and it distills almost completely, a small residue of gummy matter or of coke if the final heat has been pushed far enough being left. The distillate is called caoutchoucin. According to Mr. Greville Williams it consists of two polymeric hydrocarbons: one, caoutchin $C_{10}H_{16}$, boiling point 340° F. (171° C.); the other, isoprene C_5H_8 (in formula equal to one-half of caoutchin), boiling point 99° F. (37° C.). The mixture has a strong naptha-like odor and has won considerable reputation as being the best solvent for india rubber. How far it deserves its reputation is a matter open to discussion.

The solution of india rubber like its fusion is a vexed point. There is little question that it can be dissolved by proper treatment. Usually naptha, carbon disulphide or benzole are used as solvents, the choice being guided by motives of cheapness and efficiency.

It is worthy of remark that the formula given for caoutchoucin is the same as that of the principal constituent of oil of turpentine, and that the latter is often recommended as a solvent. Turpentine is slightly more volatile than caoutchoucin, its boiling point being 322° F. (161° C.) Other hydrocarbons have been recognized in the distillate by Bouchardat, Himly and G. Williams, varying in boiling point from 32° F. (0° C.) to 599° F. (315° C.), and in specific gravity from 0.630 to 0.921.

Although it has been spoken of as approximately

solid it does possess microscopic pores, to which its limited amount of elasticity of volume is mostly due. Thus it is found to absorb water, in which it is quite insoluble. As it does this it acts like a dry sponge and increases in volume a little, owing to dilation of these minute pores. The water absorbed may be as much as 18.7 to 26.4 per cent. with an increase of volume of the gum of $\frac{15}{1000}$ to $\frac{18}{1000}$. When it has once absorbed water it is very hard to get rid of it. Although the minute surface orifices communicate with the entire system of capillary vessels and pores, the surface pores on drying contract and seal up the absorbed water within the mass. This is a clew to the impracticability of the gatherer shipping dry rubber, and to the great difficulty the manufacturer experiences in drying his washed and sheeted stock before working it up by masticating or mixing and curing.

By proper manipulation caoutchouc may be made inelastic. This can be done by the freezing process or by keeping it stretched for two or three weeks. In this way threads can be made to extend and to remain extended to seven or eight times their original length. They can then be woven into a fabric. On gentle heating their original elasticity reappears and they contract. In this way fluted braids can be made which will have a high capacity for stretching.

The solution of caoutchouc is difficult often to bring about. We have seen that in water it swells a little without dissolving. In benzole it does the same, but swells to a greater extent, to 125 times its original volume or even more. Some authorities (*Watts*) go so far as to assert that no solvent completely dissolves it. Acting on it repeatedly with benzole or other solvent and taking care not to break up the swelled mass, from 49 to 60 per cent. of soluble matter can be extracted. On evaporation this is deposited as a ductile adherent film. The swelled up residue which remains undissolved is assumed to be the constituent giving strength and elasticity, and is only sparingly soluble. If the gum is masticated or kneaded at the temperature of boiling water a change occurs not well understood, by which its solubility is greatly increased. As solvents many liquids have been named. Oil of turpentine, caoutchoucin, coal-tar, naptha, benzole, petroleum-naptha, coal-tar-naptha, anhydrous ether, many essential oils, chloroform, bisulphide of carbon, pure, or mixed with seven or eight per cent. of alcohol, are among the solvents recommended. A mixture of fifty parts of benzole and seventy parts of rectified turpentine has been given as a solvent for twenty-six parts of the gum. Mastication before or after immersion in the solvent is to be advised. More will be said on this subject in a succeeding chapter.

Vulcanized india rubber is unaffected by changes of temperature within ordinary range. It softens a little on heating. Even hard vulcanite when heated can be bent and will retain the bend on cooling. It is exceedingly elastic with elasticity of shape but far less compressible as regards absolute change of volume than the raw gum. It melts at 392° F. (200° C.) It cannot be made to cohere, and no cement has yet been discovered that will satisfactorily unite two surfaces. It is unaffected by light, by ordinary acids and rubber solvents. In contact with the latter solvents it swells sometimes to nine times its original volume, but on heating returns to its original volume and shape. Of water it will absorb no more than four per cent. and often much less. If it is maintained at a high temperature 266° to 302° F. (130° to 150° C.) for a long time it gradually loses its flexibility, especially if in contact with metals. Often the escape of sulphuretted hydrogen may be observed under these conditions. A small admixture of coal tar operates to prevent this action.

Its composition and specific gravity vary widely as the most varied mixtures are added by the manufacturer. Its relation of carbon to hydrogen is unaffected by the mixtures added. While it may contain twenty per cent. or more of sulphur it is believed that but a very small quantity is combined with it, although the excess of sulphur or some equivalent, such as sulphide of antimony is essential to vulcanization. The combined sulphur is from one to two per cent. Some or all of the excess of sulphur is mechanically retained, and as the rubber in ordinary use is worked about, keeps escaping and forms a whitish dust upon the surface. By treatment with alkali some of the excess of sulphur can be removed when the rubber acquires the power of absorbing a little more water, up to six and four-tenths per cent.

Boiling oil of turpentine is given as its solvent.

CHAPTER IV.

THE MANUFACTURE OF MASTICATED, MIXED SHEET, AND VULCANIZED INDIA RUBBER.

The manufacture of india rubber relates to the production of two principal products. One is masticated unvulcanized sheet and thread rubber; the other is unmasticated mixed and cured rubber, otherwise vulcanized rubber. For the purposes of the rubber-stamp maker an intermediate product is required, namely, unmasticated mixed sheet which is uncured. This is really incompletely vulcanized india rubber.

It will be evident from the description to come that it is not advisable for any one without considerable apparatus to attempt to clean and to wash ("to sheet"), to masticate, or to mix india rubber. These operations are best accomplished in the factories. The partially vulcanized ("mixed sheet") or the pure masticated article are regular articles of commerce. Yet a full insight into the manipulation of india rubber can only be obtained by understanding its treatment from the gum up to the two separate lines of products we have indicated.

A third type of product is coated tissue, such as

Mackintosh. This really is a sequence of one of the other two processes and a few words will be said of it in concluding the chapter.

As the caoutchouc is received by the manufacturer it appears an utterly intractable mass. It occurs in lumps of every size, varying in color and odor, and very tough but elastic. In virtue however of the properties already described, its power of cohering when cut, and its softening when heated, it becomes amenable to treatment.

It is to some extent received in such assorted condition as to secure even grades, and then each grade may be washed by itself. It is thrown into water which is in many cases kept at the boiling point by steam-heat and left there for some hours. It absorbs some water and also softens. Some gum is so soft that it will not stand hot water. For such the water is kept cold. The purer gum floats; such pieces as have stones, dirt, iron, etc. in them, perhaps placed there purposely from fraudulent motives, sink and can be picked out for separate treatment.

The lumps are next cut up. A revolving circular knife driven by power is often used, and sometimes an ordinary knife is adopted. At this part of the operation there is frequently need for sorting, as the grades received may have inferior pieces mixed with the good. The cutting is mainly to secure good grading, and to remove concealed impurities. The gum then goes to the washing rollers, called the washer and sheeter. (See cut, p. 37.)

AND THE MANIPULATION OF RUBBER. 37

These are heavy corrugated rolls made very short, 9-18 inches in length, to prevent springing. They are grooved or corrugated and have a screw adjustment for regulating their distance apart. They are geared together so as to work in corresponding directions, like a clothes wringer or a rolling mill of any kind. The pieces of gum are fed into the

WASHER AND SHEETER.

rolls and are drawn between and through them. The friction tends to heat the gum. To prevent this and also to effect the washing, a supply of water, either hot or cold, is kept playing upon the mass. This dissolves out all soluble matter and washes away mechanically the chips, dirt, etc. which may be present. The whole operation is one of main force. The caoutchouc is torn and distended and delivered as a rough perforated sheet. It is passed repeatedly through the machine, the rollers being gradually brought closer together, or else different sets of rolls are used, set to different degrees of fineness. The wash water passes through a screen which catches any small detached fragments of gum.

Other types of machines have been introduced; the above is a representative form.

The rough sheets must now be perfectly dried, as water impairs the final product. This is done in drying rooms by steam heat, generally, at a temperature of about 90° F. (32° C.) The windows, if there are any, are painted to exclude sunlight, which operates to deteriorate raw gum. When absolutely dry the caoutchouc is removed and stacked away for use.

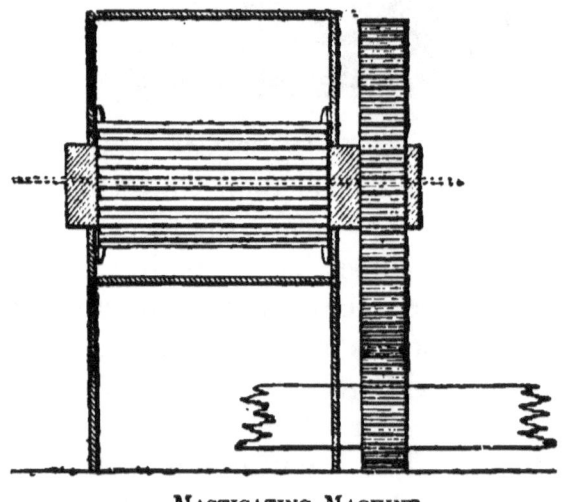

MASTICATING MACHINE.

To prepare pure gum for the manufacture of sheet rubber and as a starting point for many other preparations, the india rubber is "masticated" in special apparatus. The machine consists of a fixed cylinder within which is a corrugated roller set eccentrically and rotated by power. The perfectly dry sheets in the masticator are pressed and rolled and ground and produce a mass of even consistency. Here the welding or cohering action again appears in its fullest development. The perfect dryness of the mass enables it to keep reuniting as fast as divided. The action is assisted by the heat generated, which is not inconsiderable. Sometimes the caoutchouc is warmed before introduction, and sometimes the roller is heated by passing steam through it.

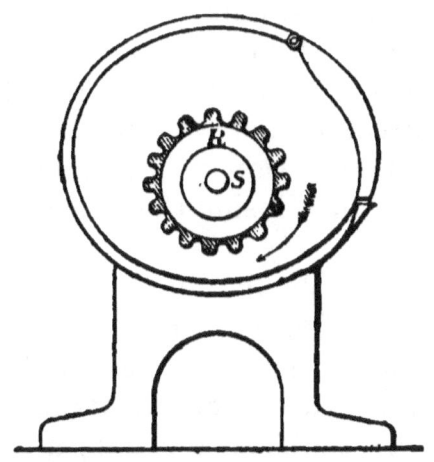

MASTICATING MACHINE.

The masticating machine the French picturesquely term the wolf (*loup*) or devil (*diable*). It is given from sixty to one hundred turns a minute, and a machine large enough to treat fifty pounds of gum in a charge, requires five horse-power to drive it. In it the sheeted gum is ultimately brought to the state of a perfectly homogeneous dark brown translucent mass.

The masticated rubber is peculiarly amenable to mechanical and chemical treatment. It can be shaped by heat and pressure, and it is the most soluble form and is used for making cement and solution, and is moulded into blocks for the manufacture of sheet and thread rubber. In the process neutral body pigments, such as oxide of zinc, or soluble transparent ones, such as alkanine may be introduced; easily decomposed matter cannot be incorporated on account of the heat.

In all these machines special provision is made to prevent any oil from getting into the gum. There is no greater enemy to india rubber than oil or fats of any description. The flanges in the masticator that roll just inside the bearing are for this purpose.

Sheet rubber is made from the blocks of masticated gum by slicing. A machine is used for the purpose which carries a knife which works back and forth in the direction of its length at high speed, making two thousand cuts a minute. The knife is kept wet by a stream of water, and about sixty cuts are made per inch. In many articles made from this sheet the marks of the cuts can be seen as a fine ribbing. The appearance is familiar to many readers.

The sheet is often cut from rectangular blocks, but cylindrical blocks are also used. The latter are rotated in front of the knife edge and a long, continuous sheet can thus be obtained.

The sheet rubber can be cut into threads on webbing and braid. Everyone has noticed that these threads are usually square. The method of preparation accounts for it. Vulcanized sheet is now almost universally used for threads.

Round threads however can be made by forcing softened or partly dissolved gum through a die.

It is from unvulcanized masticated sheet that toy balloons, tobacco pouches, etc., are made. It is the starting point for india rubber bands. For the usual form of the latter article the sheet is cemented into a long tube which is afterwards cut transversely, giving bands of any desired width. To make any of these articles satisfactory vulcanization is imperative. Unvulcanized rubber for many years was used, but it is now completely displaced by the vulcanized product. Sheet rubber is made as above; is vulcanized by some of the absorption processes described in the chapter on vulcanization.

We now come to the second product: regularly mixed and cured rubber. Its starting point is the washed india rubber from the washer and sheeter.

We have seen that the pure gum or caoutchouc is very sensitive to changes of temperature. At the freezing point of water it is hard and rigid, and at the boiling point is like putty in consistency. There are several substances which can be made to combine with the gum and which remove from it this susceptibility to change of temperature. The process of effecting this combination is called vulcanization, and the product is called vulcanized india rubber. Sulphur is the agent most generally employed.

In the factory the normal vulcanization is carried out in two steps, mixing and curing. The washed sheet india rubber which has not been masticated and which must be perfectly dry is the starting

MAKING MIXED RUBBER.

point, and the mixing rolls shown in the cuts are the mechanism for carrying out the first step. These are a pair of powerful rollers which are geared so as to work like ordinary rolls, except that one revolves about three times as fast as the other. They are heated by steam, which is introduced inside of them. The sheet is first passed through them a few times to secure its softness, and then the operative begins to sprinkle sulphur upon it as it enters the rolls. This is continued, the rubber passing and repassing until perfect incorporation is secured. About ten per cent. of sulphur is added, and a workman can take care of thirty pounds at a time.

This material is incompletely vulcanized. It is in its present condition very amenable to heat and is ready for any moulding process. Generally it is rolled out or "calendered" into sheets of different thickness from which articles are made in moulds by curing.

These sheets are of especial interest to the reader as they are the material from which most small articles are made, including rubber stamps.

This rolling of the mixed india rubber into sheets of definite thickness is done by special calendering rolls. The product is termed "mixed sheet."

In the mixing rolls the incorporation of other material is often brought about. Zinc white, lead sulphide, antimony sulphide, chalk, clay, talc, barium sulphate, plaster of paris, zinc sulphide, lead sulphate, white lead, oxides of lead, magnesia, silica, form a list of ordinary mixing ingredients. These lower the cost of the finished material and are often serious adulterants. For some cases the addition if not carried too far is not injurious, or even may be beneficial. A proper admixture renders the gum more easily moulded and treated in the shaping processes.

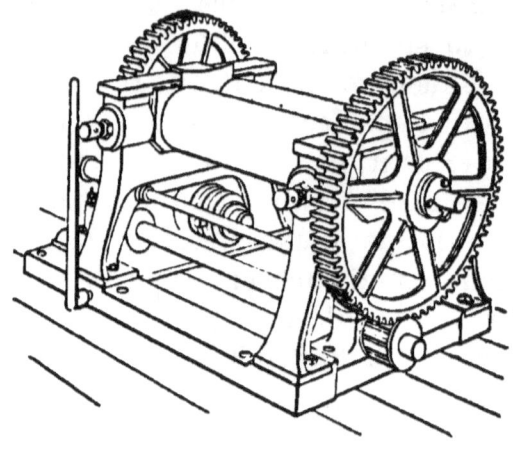

MIXING ROLLS.

The next step in the vulcanizing process is the heating of the mass, which step is called "curing." Up to a temperature in the neighborhood of that of boiling water the mixed rubber can be heated without change except as it is softened. But if the heat is increased it begins to get a little more elastic and less doughy, and eventually becomes "cured" or vulcanized. The temperature for vulcanization is about 284° F. (140° C.). The word "about" is used advisedly, for it is not only a question of heat but of time of exposure. After vulcanizing, including the curing, india rubber cannot be moulded to any great extent. In the manufacturing process, therefore, it is before curing placed in the moulds, heated, shaped by pressure, and by exposure to a higher heat in a steam oven called a vulcanizer, is at once cured.

To prevent adherence to the moulds they are dusted over with ground soapstone, and the rubber itself is often thus coated.

The methods of vulcanization and curing, which may be of special use to the reader, are given in the chapters devoted to that subject (chapter XI.), and in the one devoted to rubber stamps.

Hard rubber, termed ebonite when black, and vulcanite when of other colors, is simply vulcanized rubber containing a large percentage of sulphur added in the mixing process.

The manufacture of coated tissues is effected in several ways. The following is a typical process. A mixture of one part washed and sheeted india rubber with one part zinc white, one fourth part sulphur, and about one third part naptha is mixed into a dough-like mass and is spread upon the cloth by machinery. The latter is simple. It consists of a bare board arranged to move under a scraping bar. The cloth is placed on the board and carried under the bar. The coating mixture is fed on one side of the bar upon the surface of the cloth. As it passes under, a regulated amount, according to the set of the bar, adheres. It is then dried by steam heat and recoated, until ordinarily six coats, each about one one-hundreth of an inch in thickness, have been given. Three coats are given in each direction with intermediate drying. The fabric is then cured by heat in vulcanizers.

Sometimes the sulphur is omitted from the mixture and cold curing, as described later, is adopted. When the goods are made up the seams are secured with rubber cement, a thick solution of masticated gum. Such seams have to be vulcanized.

Sometimes two such fabrics before curing or vulcanization, are placed face to face and allowed to adhere and are then cured or vulcanized.

Enough has been said in this outline of the manufacturer's treatment of india rubber to show that the first treatment requires machinery. Very little can be done with mortar and pestle, although in making up solution these simple instrumentalities are available. As a starting point for making small articles masticated sheet rubber and mixed sheet rubber are the staple materials. The preceding steps are best accomplished in the factory.

CHAPTER V.

INDIA RUBBER STAMP MAKING.

We have seen that india rubber cannot be cast in moulds. Except in special cases deposition from solution is not available. It has to be shaped by a combination of heat and pressure. When gently heated it softens and can be pressed in a mould. As it cools it retains the shape thus given and is moulded. This applies to all unvulcanized india rubber. If mixed rubber is moulded and heated to a higher temperature without removal from the mould the curing process is brought about and the rubber may be not only moulded but cured and the product is moulded vulcanized india rubber. The mixed sheet whose manufacture is described in chapter IV. (page 42) is the starting point in rubber stamp making. It is made for this purpose by the manufacturers.

When the material is examined it looks like ordinary white india rubber, being firm in texture and quite strong. On heating to 280° F. to 290° F. (137° C. to 143° C.) it begins to become "cured," and if in a thin sheet one to ten minutes are sufficient for the process. As the heat is applied the india rubber first softens and becomes much like putty. It can now be pressed through the smallest orifice and will fill up the finest details of anything it is pressed against. It is at this point that pressure must be applied to drive it into the interstices of the mould.

As the heat continues it begins to lose its doughy or putty-like consistency. This marks the reaction of the vulcanizing materials. They gradually combine with and change the nature of the caoutchouc. The rubber while still quite soft is elastic. If pressed by the point of a knife it yields, but springs back to its shape when released from pressure. The india rubber is vulcanized.

On removal from the mould it will be found to reproduce its smallest detail. The color and appearance have not changed much, but its nature and properties are now those of vulcanized rubber. It is unaffected by heat or cold within ordinary ranges of temperature, and if the india rubber is of good quality and made by a proper formula it will last for years.

The first thing to be described is the mould, which includes the arrangements for pressing the sheet of india rubber while heated. A small press is needed for this purpose. It may be of the simplest description, and as an example of a homemade but perfectly efficient one the illustration may be referred to. The base of the press is a piece of iron, if heat is to be directly employed. Where a

AND THE MANIPULATION OF RUBBER. 49

chamber vulcanizer is used both base and platen may be of wood. But from every point of view iron is the best. It lasts forever, admits of direct heating, and does not split, warp, or char. Through two holes drilled near its opposite sides two ordinary bolts are thrust. It is best to use flat headed bolts, and to countersink a recess for the

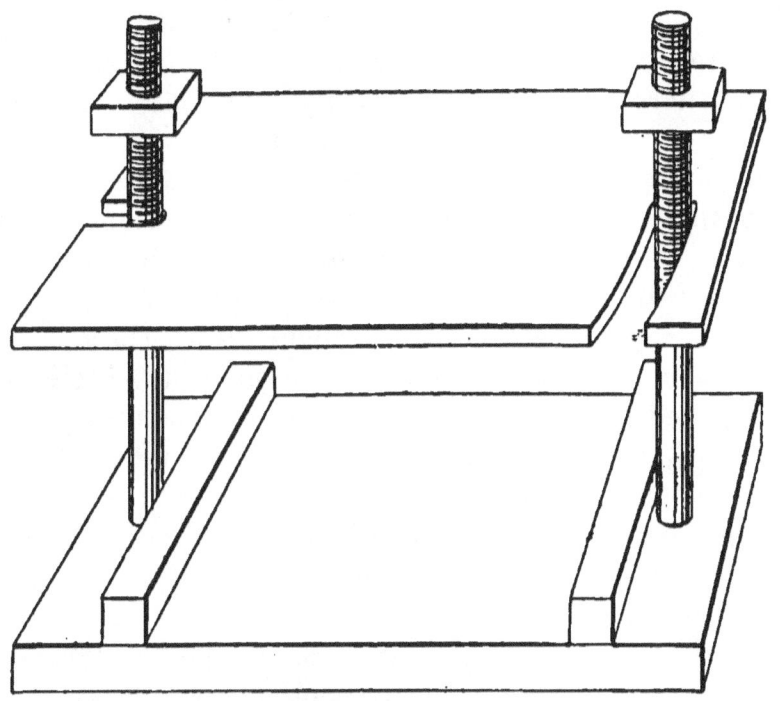

SIMPLE VULCANIZING PRESS FOR RUBBER STAMPS.

heads in order to keep the bottom level. The heads may need to be filed off so as to reduce their thickness, in order to secure this object. The bolts may be soldered in place. One thing should be carefully watched for—the bolts should be set true so as to rise vertically from the plane of the base.

The platen is best made of iron, cut of the shape shown. This is an excellent disposition of the screw-bolt slots, as by swinging the right end of the platen back it can be taken off without removing the nuts and lifting it over the ends of the screws. Besides the two nuts fitting the thread of the screws it is well to have half a dozen extra ones larger than the others, which will slip easily over the bolts, so as to act as washers. The object of these is to adapt the press to objects of different thickness. The thread upon an ordinary bolt does not extend clear to the head, but by slipping on some loose nuts the plates can be forced together if desired.

This press can be simplified. Both base and platen can be made of wood, the platen being simply bored for the bolts, and the latter driven tightly through the holes in the base so as to retain their place. Even this can be improved on as regards simplicity. Two blocks of wood screwed together by two or more long wood screws may be made to do efficient work.

One trouble is apparent with all these devices, and that is the want of parallelism of the opposed planes. The base and platen may be true and parallel or they may not. Perhaps the simplest way of securing this is the best. It consists in placing across the base two distance pieces, which may be slips of wood. These must have perfectly parallel faces. As the press is screwed up they will be gripped between the platen and base and will not only ensure their parallelism but will keep them at an exact distance apart. Such distance pieces are shown in the same cut. Pieces of printers' "furniture," spaces, or "quads," may be used for this purpose. They should not be fastened in place if there is need to adapt the press to more than one thickness of material and matrix.

The above described apparatus is a vulcanizing press. A further improvement in it may be effected by the use of spring pressure. Two strong spiral springs may be dropped over the bolts, the nuts being screwed on above them, or a powerful spring of flat brass or steel ribband bent into the shape of a shallow letter V may intervene between nuts and platen, the centre of the bend bearing against the centre of the platen.

As regards the strength of the springs there is this to be said. The distance pieces will prevent a spring that would ordinarily be too powerful from doing any harm. Such distance pieces should be used, as the springs must be based upon giving a pressure of many pounds per square inch of surface to be acted on. They should have a range of an eighth of an inch or more. The greater the range the more evenly will they work.

The next cut shows an excellent little screw press, that is made for the purpose of pressing vulcanizing flasks. This is so simple that it will suggest to the mechanical reader how he can make a single-screw press, which is by far the most convenient to use. In the stationery stores very small model cast iron copying presses designed for use as paper weights are sold. They are excellent for a limited amount of small sized work.

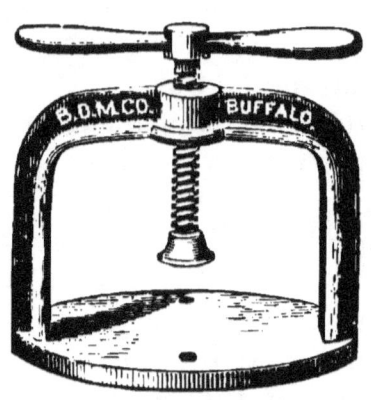

VULCANIZING FLASK CLAMP.

A large sized gas heated press, such as made for the purpose of manufacturing rubber stamps, is shown in the next cut, p. 53. Its construction is obvious. It is termed by the trade a vulcanizer. Its manipulation will be given further on.

Type are generally the object to be copied. These are best set up with high quads and spaces. Naturally rather a large type is chosen, with extra wide spaces between the letters. Some advise rubbing the type faces full of hard soap, afterwards brushing off the face, leaving the hollows filled. Sometimes wax is recommended for the same purpose. This prevents the plaster of the matrix entering so deeply into the cavities of the letters.

The type forming the model to be reproduced, is locked in a frame. Two pieces of printers' furni-

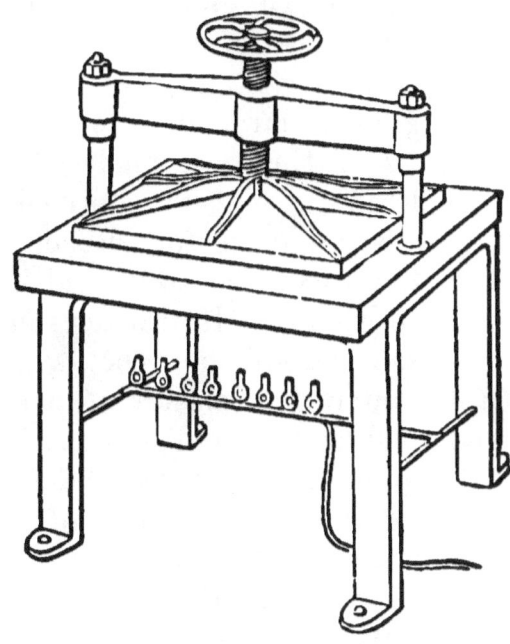

GAS-HEATED STAMP VULCANIZER.

ture or other wooden strips screwed together by wood screws at their ends will answer for a locking frame for small inscriptions.

The model to be copied need not be type, but any desired relief may be used, such as an electrotype, a stereotype, an engraving or another rubber stamp. In any case it is to be placed upon a flat surface, best an "imposing stone" or piece of marble, with the inscription upwards. On each side of it distance pieces reaching about one-eighth inch above its upper surface are to be placed.

The next shaping appliance is the matrix or mould, or reverse of the model which is to be copied. This in the case of rubber stamps is properly called the matrix. Those who have witnessed the stereotyping of a large daily newspaper have seen the matrices of the type made of paper and paste, the whole mixture being termed "flong." Such a matrix is required for rubber type, but paper is rather too susceptible to heat although good work can be done with it. It also does not enter as deeply into the cavities of the type as is desirable. As a rule a fine quality of plaster of paris is to be recommended. What is sold as dental plaster is the best, but common plaster can be used. It is mixed with water or with a solution of gum arabic or dextrine in water. For the latter enough gum should be added to make the mixing solution as thick as thin syrup.

A piece of iron, perfectly flat and true, is now to be taken, large enough to more than cover the inscription to be copied. Upon its surface a putty made of the plaster and the liquid used in mixing is to be spread. This should be rather stiff. The surface of the iron should not be too smooth as it is desirable that the plaster should adhere well on setting. The plaster should be smoothly spread to a depth of three-sixteenths or a quarter of an inch.

It is best applied with a palette knife or trowel, although a table knife will answer perfectly. If its surface does not become smooth it can be made so by applying a little of the solution with the knife or trowel.

Before this has been done the model must be oiled. Olive oil or other clear oil is applied to all parts of the type faces, and the excess is then wiped off and cleared out of the interstices with a piece of blotting paper.

Next the plate with the plaster is inverted and is pressed steadily down upon the model until it strikes the distance pieces. It is left to set. In about ten minutes it can be raised, when it will be found to give a beautiful impression true to the smallest detail of each letter.

It has been said that water may be used as the mixing fluid. If this is done it is well to strengthen the mould by saturating it with an alcoholic solution of shellac, after it has dried thoroughly, best for a few hours in an oven. This operates to strengthen the small projections that are liable to crumble or to break off in use.

The dealers in rubber stamp supplies sell a lever press for conducting the operation of producing the matrix. The type is locked in a special chase, which is carried on a bed that travels under and out from under the platen of the press upon rollers. From each corner of the chase in which the type model is locked, a pin rises which is encircled by a spiral spring. A square frame of flat iron with holes at the corners for the pins to pass through, rests upon these springs well above the type. The pins pass through holes in its corners. The matrix plate with its coating of plaster is placed upon this frame, which supports it above and not touching the type. The whole is now rolled under the press and the lever pulled to produce the impression. As the pressure is released the frame with the matrix is raised from the type by the action of the springs. This can be done immediately, and before the plaster has set. It is almost impossible to raise it by hand with the requisite steadiness. The same chase with corner pins and springs can be used in a screw press, the one press answering for making the matrix and for moulding and curing the stamps. The plaster matrix can also be made by casting from a thinner mixture of plaster and water. After the type has been set up, or the model has been selected and placed face up and horizontal, a little ridge or projection must be made all around it. Paper can be pasted around it, and wound with thread for this purpose. It is oiled and wiped off as before. The plaster is now mixed with water to the consistency of cream, and is poured upon the model until it lies even with the projecting ledges or paper border. In an hour or less it can be removed. If water is used the mould should before use be treated with shellac solution as already described. The plaster may also be mixed with gum arabic solution, or with three to ten per cent. of powdered marshmallow root. This increases its toughness.

What is known as the oxychloride of zinc cement appears to the author to be far preferable to common plaster of paris. It is a trifle more expensive, but it costs so little that it is well worth trying. It is made by mixing oxide of zinc with a solution of zinc chloride. No particular strength of solution or proportions are prescribed; the zinc chloride solution should be a strong one, and the mixture should be of about the consistency of soft putty.

Zinc chloride may be bought as a solid substance or in strong solution. The latter answers for the mixing directly. It may also be simply made by dissolving metallic zinc in strong hydrochloric acid. The manipulation is exactly the same as with plaster of paris.

The manufacture of papier maché and of other matrices is given in a special chapter. For all ordinary purposes the plaster or cement matrices are ample.

The stamp is made from the mixed uncured sheet rubber, whose preparation in the factory, including the operation of calendering it into sheets, has already been described. The best advice the reader can be given is not to attempt to make it except as a matter of interest and experiment. It can be purchased especially prepared for stamps from the dealers in india rubber.

A piece is cut from the sheet large enough to cover the face of the matrix. It should have a perfectly smooth surface, without cloth wrapper marks sometimes found impressed on it. The sheet as received from the maker is about one-eighth of an inch thick. It is thrown into a box of powdered soapstone or talc to secure a coating of the same on both sides. A little is dusted over the matrix and the excess is blown off. The matrix is now placed upon the base of the press, and heat is applied.

To carry out the process most simply the press if of metal may be placed upon a support over a gas burner or kerosene lamp, or even on a kitchen range or stove. It will in a few minutes become warm. The sheet of india rubber is now dusted off and is placed in the press upon the matrix. The platen of the press is screwed down upon it.

As the india rubber becomes hot it begins to soften and flow. By the action of the screw of the press it must be forced down from time to time as it softens. This drives the putty-like material into all the interstices of the mould. The excess escapes from the sides of the tympan in cases where the latter is of restricted area. The press theoretically should be heated to the vulcanizing temperature, which is 284° F. (140° C.). In practice the heat is not determined with a thermometer. The operator learns by experience how much heat to apply. The regulation type of gas heated press or stamp vulcanizer is shown in the illustration on page 53.

As some of the india rubber is sure to protrude, the progress of the work can be watched from its action. By pressing the point of a knife against it the period of vulcanization can be told. Before the material is heated it is elastic and resists the

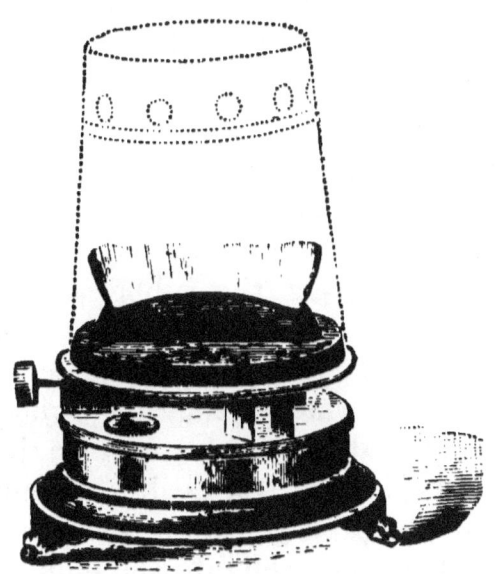

OIL STOVE FOR HEATING VULCANIZERS.

pressure of the knife; as heat is applied it becomes soft like putty; as the heat increases it again stiffens and becomes quite elastic. At this point the press can be opened and the sheet and matrix can be taken out or the platen swung aside. On pulling or stripping the sheet from the matrix it will be found to reproduce the model in elastic india rubber to the minutest detail.

As regards the minor details there is something

to be said. Distance pieces to gauge the thickness have been recommended for the home-made press, page 48. Care must be taken to have these low enough to provide for enough excess of material to produce a good impression. For ordinary stamp work they should allow about one-sixteenth of an inch for the "squeeze." It will be seen that by using the distance or gauge pieces both for making the matrix and for moulding and curing the stamp, absolute parallelism of surfaces will be secured.

The reader will have noticed in the description and will find at once in practice that the press has to be screwed up as the rubber softens. Where heavy iron presses are used the large mass of heated iron comprised in the platen of the press instantly heats the upper surface of the india rubber sheet and the heat immediately penetrates into it, while the heated matrix heats it from below. Thus it softens at once, and the press is directly turned down and the india rubber is driven into the mould and curing at once begins. But where small presses are used this manipulation is not so easy. For such the springs mentioned on page 51, are highly to be recommended. The matrix and india rubber can be put into the cold press, and the tympan with intervening springs can be screwed down so as to compress them. Then on applying heat the moulding takes place automatically.

With a hot press and good sheet a period of three to ten minutes is ample for moulding and curing.

Instead of sprinkling with talc the matrix may be oiled and sprinkled with plumbago and afterwards polished with a brush. This is not so clean a material as talc and is not to be recommended for general use, especially as oil is a bad substance to bring in contact with rubber.

The distance or gauge pieces whose use has been recommended are not necessary where presses working truly parallel as regards their opposing faces are used. But where home-made apparatus is used they will be found a valuable addition.

In describing the simple press it was said that it could be made of wood. It is evident that a wooden press could not be used for direct heating. Such a press must be used in a hot chamber or vulcanizer, properly so called. Originally rubber stamps were generally made in chamber vulcanizers.

The next cut shows a combined matrix making, moulding and vulcanizing apparatus of very convenient and compact form and adapted for rapid work. As the press stands in the cut the matrix press is seen in front. A box or chase is carried under its platen by two trunnions, so as to be free to oscillate to a limited extent. The type model is secured in this box. Above this box or chase is a cross-bar with screw and platen attached, connected at will to two standards or pillars, so as to constitute the matrix press.

A matrix plate swings on a hinge joint between the two presses. The hinge-pin is removable. Its ends can be seen projecting to right and left of the press columns. The hinge is at such a height that when the matrix plate is swung forward over the type box it will rest upon it in a nearly horizontal position. The pivoted box will adjust itself so as to come into parallelism with the plate.

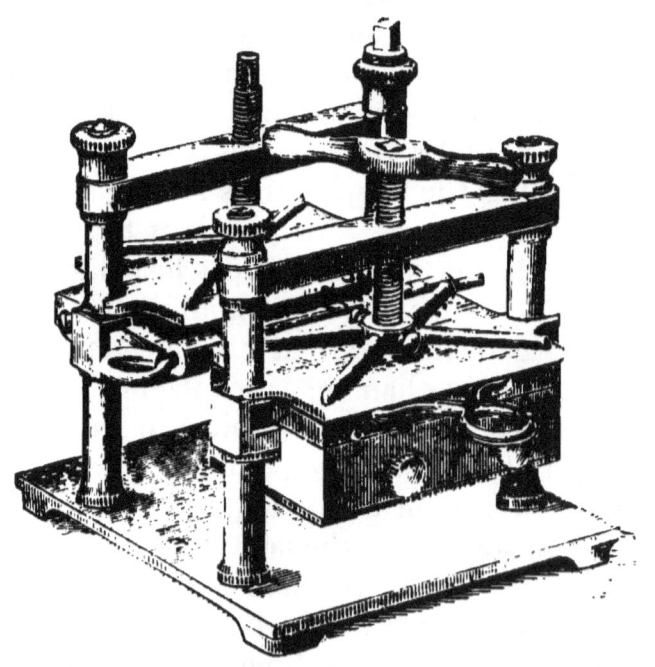

MATRIX MAKING, MOULDING AND VULCANIZING APPARATUS.

When the matrix plate is swung back it falls upon the base plate of the vulcanizing press seen in the rear.

In use the composition used for the matrix is spread upon the matrix plate, which may for this purpose be removed from the apparatus. It is replaced and the hinge-pin is pushed home. This is done with the composition coated side facing the front of the apparatus as it stands in the cut. The plate is then swung forwards, the platen of the matrix press being turned forward out of the way, and is pressed down upon the type or other model that rests in the type box. If desired the press is used to force it home. The cross-bars of both the presses are arranged to swing each one on one of the pillars, so that the platens are turned to one side out of the way of the matrix plate as it is swung back and forth.

The pressure is released and the platens are turned aside. The matrix plate is swung over to the rear upon the bed-plate of the vulcanizing press. Here it lies with the composition-matrix upwards.

A lighted lamp, either alcohol or gas, is placed beneath the bed-plate of the vulcanizing press on which the matrix rests. This quickly dries it and brings it to a good curing temperature. The cross-bar and platen may be swung over it during the heating so as to be heated at the same time. The matrix is talced when dry and hot; the mixed sheet itself talced, is placed upon the matrix, the platen is screwed down upon it, and in a minute or two the moulding and curing is completed.

A vulcanizer, properly speaking, is a vessel arranged to heat to a definite degree any desired arti-

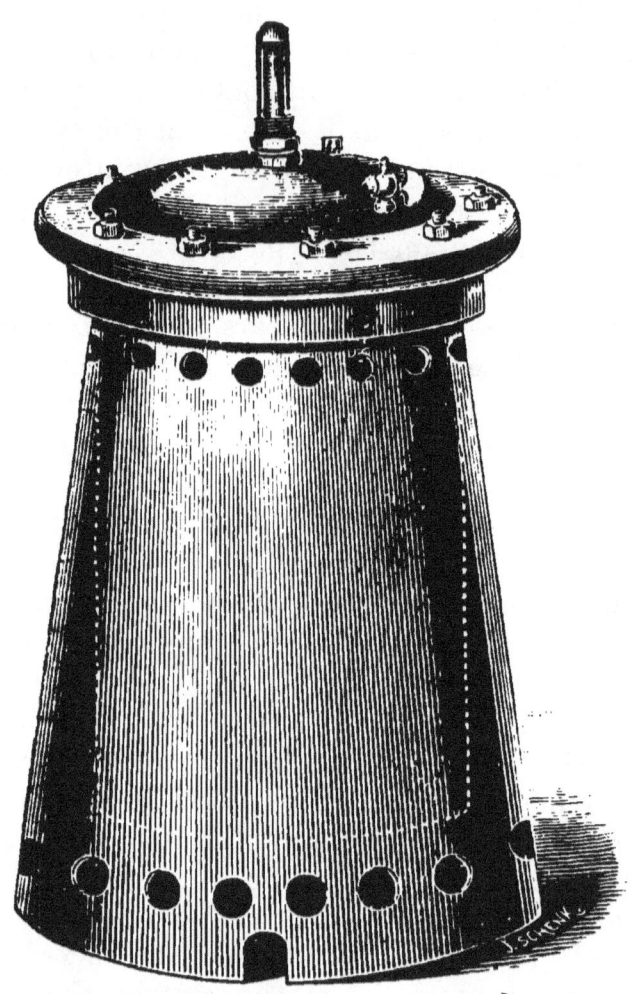

RUBBER STAMP VULCANIZER.

cles which are to be cured. The favorite type have been the steam vulcanizers. If steam is generated from water at a constant pressure, other things being equal a constant temperature will be produced. By raising or lowering the pressure the temperature can be made to rise or fall. A steam vulcanizer is a tightly sealed vessel which contains water and which is provided with a thermometer or a pressure gauge as well as a safety-valve, safety disc or safety plug. By keeping the gauge at constant pressure or by keeping the thermometer constant the temperature can be limited and kept steady. The following table gives some pressure in pounds per square inch with temperatures corresponding to steam of such pressures:

Lbs. per square inch.	Temp. Fahr.	Temp. Cent.
45.512	275°	135°
52.548	284°	140°
60.442	293°	145°
67.408	300.2°	149°

The illustration, p. 64, shows a vulcanizer of modern type made for rubber stamp work. In some recent vulcanizers the water and steam are excluded from the vulcanizing chamber, being contained within double walls forming a steam jacket and maintaining a constant heat within the chamber. These illustrate a point that has been much misapprehended, namely that curing is independent of pressure or atmosphere. Because vulcanizers have generally been filled with steam at high pressure many have supposed that the steam or pressure had something to do with their action. The fact is that it is only the heat due to the steam at such pressure that is instrumental. Steam is a very powerful radiator and absorber of so called radiant heat. For this reason an atmosphere of steam maintains all

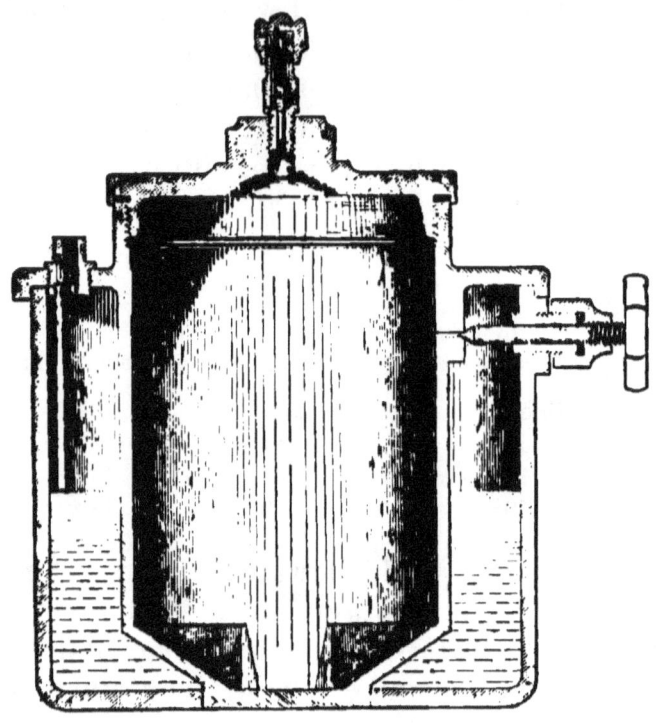

STEAM JACKET VULCANIZER.

parts of the vulcanizer at an even temperature and is to that extent advantageous. Its presence and the pressure it generates are not by any means required for vulcanizing. Its pressure is entirely without effect.

To use a steam vulcanizer, water is introduced,

the article in the press or mould is placed in it, and the top is secured. Heat is then applied, best if on the small scale, from a Bunsen gas burner gas, or oil stove. Either the pressure gauge or thermometer may be watched, and the flame turned up or down to keep it at the proper temperature.

Moulding cannot be executed in the ordinary closed chambers. The press must first be heated to the temperature of boiling water or thereabouts and the moulding is then effected by screwing down the mould screw, upon the sheet and matrix. It is then placed in the vulcanizer and cured.

The manufacturers supply gas regulators which automatically regulate the gas supply. These are worked by the steam pressure. If any one wishes to study the practical manipulation of small steam vulcanizers he can see them in use at any dentist's office.

There is no need of a steam vulcanizer for ordinary stamp work. The hot press system already described answers every purpose and is in use by the most advanced manufacturers for thin sheet work. But if a wooden moulding press is used then it must be heated in a vulcanizer or some kind of oven or hot chamber.

A very simple and reasonably satisfactory oven or air bath can be made from a flower pot and a couple of tin plates. A plate larger in diameter than the mouth of the flower pot forms the base of the apparatus. This is supported on a stand over the gas lamp or other source of heat. A smokeless flame or one depositing no lampblack should be used. Alcohol or a kerosene oil stove illustrated on page 59 are excellent. On this plate a smaller plate is inverted, which latter must be so small as to be surrounded by the flower pot and to be included within it when the pot is placed over it like an extinguisher.

FLOWER POT VULCANIZER ON STAND.

A chemical or round stemmed thermometer is arranged to go through the aperture in the upturned bottom of the pot. This may be hung from a support or it may be secured by passing through a hole in a cork or block of wood. Its bulb should be near the part of the chamber to be occupied by the mould or press.

The press with the article to be cured is placed upon the inner plate. The temperature is maintained at the proper point by regulating the heat, and all the conditions for excellent work are supplied. The disposition of the apparatus is shown in the cuts.

INTERIOR OF FLOWER POT VULCANIZER.

Another arrangement equally simple is given in the next cut. An iron kettle has a layer of type metal or lead poured an inch thick cast within it upon its bottom. A thermometer passing through a hole in the cover enters a cup of glycerine that stands upon the bottom. This gives the temperature.

The object of having a thick or a double bottom is to prevent excessive radiation of heat from any one part. The essential condition for good operation is to maintain an even temperature throughout the chamber.

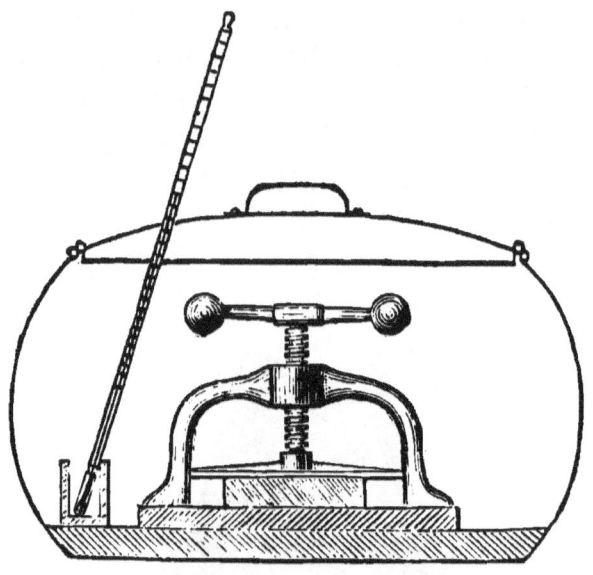

FISH KETTLE VULCANIZER.

The thermometer is not an absolute necessity. By removing the press from time to time and inspecting the overflow of india rubber the progress of the operation can be watched. An extra piece of india rubber may be placed on a piece of wood by the side of or upon the wooden portion of the press, and its condition can be taken as the criterion. Pressure with the point of a knife will tell the vulcanizing point.

By the press system of curing, a heat far above the vulcanizing temperature may be made to do good work by a very short application. There is however danger of burning the work if left in too long. If the air-bath with thermometer or the steam vulcanizer is used, and the heat is kept down to the proper curing temperature, there is no danger of burning the india rubber even if the curing is considerably prolonged.

As the flower pot has often to be lifted off for introduction or removal of the press, and as it gets quite hot, a holder of some kind is requisite. A piece of heavy blotting paper is very convenient for this purpose.

The flower pot system with thermometer can be further simplified by being used on a stove or range. A china saucer inverted, or some similar support, should be placed under the pot. A part of the stove at very low heat will suffice. The kettle vulcanizer, can also be placed on a stove so as to dispense with gas or oil.

Finally, as the last step in simplifying the work, a stamp can be made without any special apparatus beyond a hot flat iron. The matrix may be placed on a stove where the heat is rather low, the talc-coated mixed rubber sheet placed upon it, and on this a hot flat iron. In a few minutes if the heat is sufficient the stamp will be finished.

A few words may be said about the type. High spaces and quads between the letters should be used, such as will come up to the shoulder of the type, as has been said. But a very nice effect is produced by using low quads between words. This leaves each word elevated by itself, producing a good appearance.

Autograph stamps are made from a model cut in wood by a wood engraver. The autograph is written in some form of copying ink upon a piece of paper, and is transferred by moistening and. pressure to a block of wood. With an engraver's tool the wood is cut away from the lines, as the block is routed after the inscription has been "outlined." The woodcut is used as a model for making a matrix.

It is evident that an autograph of fair quality could be obtained from a chalk plate. But in rubber stamp work to get good results certain essential parts should be of the best. These parts include the mixed rubber, model and matrix. A departure from excellence in any of these tends to the production of an inferior stamp. What is known as a "healthy cure" is above all essential to the appearance of the product.

The stamp thus made is attached to a wooden handle by common glue or by one of the rubber cements given in chapter XVI.

CHAPTER VI.

INDIA RUBBER TYPE MAKING.

INDIA rubber type are often used to set up different inscriptions in wooden handles, or different date figures in rubber stamps. The latter are in such cases made with slots or recesses to receive them. Rubber type are much shorter than regular type, and as a rule are larger in the body in proportion to the face of the letter. Where only a few are required the following process is the simplest way of making them from mixed rubber sheet.

The type which are to be copied are set up on a level base or imposing stone, and quads or spaces are put between them. High quads and spaces should be used; otherwise they should be pushed up until even with the shoulders of the type. After oiling the faces a matrix is produced exactly as described for stamps. Before it has set quite hard the plaster or cement is cut off so that it will just fit within a little " flask " or frame.

The latter may be made of tin or wood and may be rectangular or circular, provided it is large enough to include within its area the full working face of the matrix. It should be about half an inch or five-eighths of an inch deep. Its object is to prevent the softened india rubber from spreading, so as to secure the requisite height of the type produced.

A piece of wood or metal is cut so as to fit closely within this frame like a plunger. It is provided with shoulders or cross pieces, so as to limit the depth to which it can be inserted. It will be seen that when matrix, flask, and plunger are all put together a complete mould for a block of type is

India Rubber Type Mould.

produced, as shown in the illustration, the matrix with its plate forming the bottom of the box. After the flask is placed upon the matrix it is filled with the mixed uncured india rubber sheet. As a matter of preference thick sheet is used, but scraps of all shapes can be employed as it all fuses together. The mould and matrix are of course first well dusted with talc powder. The plunger is put on and the whole is pressed. Heat is next applied in a vulcanizer or hot air chamber, such as the flower pot arrangement, or in boiling water. As the sheet reaches the boiling point 212° F. (100° C.) the flask is removed and the plunger examined. If it goes down to its seat without expelling any india rubber more of the latter is required and is accordingly inserted, the plunger being taken off for the purpose. The softened gum should ooze out around the sides of the plunger. The whole is again put under pressure, and the platen is screwed down, and if all is right an excess of rubber showing itself, the whole is put in the hot chamber, the heat is raised to 284° F. (140° C.), and is maintained there for half an hour.

It is almost a necessity to secure the matrix plate to the bottom of the flask. This for a single operation may be done by screws, or for several operations by hooks or catches.

When the curing is complete the mould is removed from the vulcanizer, is allowed to cool and is opened. The block of type will come out with perfect reproduction of the letters upon one side. If all the directions have been followed as regards distance pieces, level imposing surface, etc., both faces will be exactly parallel, and any number of other blocks can be reproduced of exactly the same height, not necessarily from the same matrix, although one good matrix can be used many times.

The type have now to be cut apart. This is done with a sharp knife which is kept wet. It is worked with a sawing motion, and if sharp and properly used will cut with regularity, and smoothly. Type with knife marks on the sides are always unmechanical in appearance and seem to be "home made."

The object of using high quads and spaces or of pushing them up, will now be evident. It secures the evenness of the general face of the block of letters, which otherwise would have a deep depression between each pair of letters. If the quads and leads are properly arranged, the letters will project upwards from a smooth, plane surface.

The dealers in rubber stamp maker's supplies sell special steel moulds for the purpose of making them. This does away with all necessity for making matrices, and making up a flask, etc. The general manipulation is that given above. Where many are to be made the regular mould is by all means to be recommended.

Sometimes type are made by cementing single letters made by the stamp process upon wooden bodies.

CHAPTER VII.

THE MAKING OF STAMPS AND TYPE FROM VULCANIZED INDIA RUBBER.

Although all reference hitherto in the matters of stamps and type has been to their manufacture from uncured india rubber, a good deal can be done with vulcanized and cured gum. The stock that is known in the trade as pure gum, such as is used for bicycle tyres, for steam packing and the like, can be made to yield to moulding to a certain degree. It will not flow and unite as will the uncured gum, but it is evident that in certain cases its stiffness is even an advantage. Thus with it, rubber type can be made without any flask or frame. The material has stiffness enough to support itself.

The manipulation is of the simplest. A piece is cut out with a knife so as to be of proper thickness and size. It should be a little thicker than will ultimately be required. The two opposite surfaces should be smooth and parallel. It is talced, and placed in the press with the matrix beneath it, and subjected to pressure by the screws being turned down. It is then placed in the vulcanizing chamber and heated to about 284° F. (140° C.).

After it has become hot it softens a little. The press is removed from the hot chamber and is again screwed down as hard as the matrix can stand. This point is largely a matter of judgment. The heat is largely indifferent as long as it is anywhere near the above temperature.

By one or two repetitions of the pressing and heating the softened india rubber can be made to take quite a deep impression from a suitable matrix. It is allowed to cool under full pressure. When removed from the press, it will retain the characters.

It is evident that impressions in as high relief or as deep and clear as those yielded by uncured india rubber need not be expected. But where the other cannot be had, or where some experimental or temporary work only is on hand, this process will be very convenient.

The material may be half an inch thick. From such india rubber type can be cut with advantage.

Old rubber can be thus used. The writer has obtained excellent results from pieces of an old discarded bicycle tyre.

The great point is to apply a heavy pressure to the hot material. Many other articles can be thus produced extemporaneously. At the same time it must be considered only a makeshift. One who has used the soft, easy flowing uncured gum would never be reconciled to the use of so rigid and difficultly moulded a material, one too that can never be trusted to reproduce intricate moulds of considerable depth. In the slow yielding of the half melted uncured gum, so amenable to slight pressure, a quality of availability is found that is missed in the other. One is worked by main force where the other readily yields and takes the most complicated shapes.

By the above process stamps of such thickness may be made that they can be used without handles. It is also useful for impressing a designation of any kind upon ready cured articles. It suggests a very useful department of manipulation of india rubber.

The heating and moulding can be done also in a hot liquid bath such as described in chapter XI.

CHAPTER VIII.

VARIOUS TYPE MATRICES FOR RUBBER STAMPS AND TYPES.

Matrices for stamp moulds can be made by several of the methods used by stereotypers. Thus an electrotype could be taken directly from the face of the type. There would be little or no utility in doing this where the simpler processes are available.

PAPIER MACHÉ MATRICES.

The stereotyper for daily newspaper work uses very generally the papier maché or "flong" process of reproducing the page. This is also available for rubber stamp making.

The first requirement is paste. This is made by softening twelve parts of whiting in forty parts of water, letting it soak for an hour or more. Nine parts of wheat flour are added. This is best mixed with a little water before adding to the main mixture. It is then brought to the boil and seven parts of glue softened by soaking in twenty-one parts of water, are added. For each gallon of such mixture, one ounce of white crystallized carbolic acid is added if it is to be kept for a long time.

The "flong" is made by pasting together, one on top of the other, a sheet of fine hard tissue paper, three sheets of blotting paper (about 23 pounds to the ream), and a heavy sheet of manilla paper. The pasting must be smooth and each layer must be pressed and rubbed down, but not too hard. It is very important to secure perfect smoothness and regularity, and entire absence of air bubbles.

Every printing office where the process is used has its own traditions as to the preparation of flong. As a great deal depends on manipulation, it would be well to endeavor to inspect its practical use in a newspaper printing office before making it. Ready prepared flong can also be procured.

The form of type must be very clean and there must be no paste on the tissue paper face of the flong. The type are lightly oiled, some powdered talc is dusted over the damp tissue paper face of the flong, and the mass is laid face downward on the type. With a stiff haired brush the paper is now beaten down against the type. Great care must be taken to beat vertically; a slight side action will ruin the resulting matrix. If the brown paper will not stand the beating, a cloth may be spread over it.

The progress of the work can be watched by raising up a corner from time to time. When sufficiently deep the last touch is given by the printer's planer. This is a block of hard wood. It is placed upon the back of the flong and is hammered down. The operation is repeated until the entire area has been treated. For much rubber stamp work the area would be so restricted that shifting would be unnecessary.

The work is then put into a heated screw press, such as the vulcanizing and matrix press, and is dried for a period varying from some minutes up to half an hour. Some blotting paper is advantageously pressed on top of the whole in the press while drying. The press is opened, the flong removed, and dried in an oven. It is kept under a piece of wire net while drying to keep it flat. The net may be of wire, .064 inch thick, with six meshes to the inch. This baking is not strictly necessary for rubber stamp work.

This gives a matrix which may be used as rubber stamp moulds. In use it is recomended to place a piece of smooth tin foil over it. This tends to give a smoother surface to the rubber.

STRUCK UP MATRICES.

Didot's polytype process may be advantageously used for producing type metal matrices. The following is the method of applying it.

The type form is firmly locked and is backed up by and secured to a solid block of wood. It is suspended in a sort of gallows frame with the face of the type downward and exactly level a few inches above a table. Underneath it a shallow tray is placed, into which some melted type metal is poured. The melted metal is carefully watched. The block and type are held by a catch so as to be released at will. Just as the type metal is on the point of solidifying, the block is released and drops upon the metal in the tray. The type should be slightly oiled. The force of the blow produces a matrix in the metal, and the form can at once be removed.

It is well to have accurately adjusted distance pieces for corresponding striking pieces on the type block to impinge upon. The process is highly spoken of, especially for small forms such as those mostly required for rubber stamps.

CHALK PLATES.

The base for this form of matrix is a metal plate whose surface is slightly roughened with sandpaper. It is next rubbed over with white of egg, and flooded with the chalk wash made as follows: Flong paste (described under Papier Maché Matrices, page 80), six ounces; whiting, twenty-four ounces; water, three pints. The whiting is softened by soaking for an hour or more. The whole must be intimately mixed. It should cover the plate to the depth of one-thirtieth to one-twentieth of an inch. The plate is dried in a perfectly horizontal position.

When dry the design or writing, etc., is made with a smooth steel point, the lines being carried clear through the white layer to the metal. The mould is now baked at a temperature well above boiling water; as high as $392°$ F. ($200°$ C.) may be reached without harm.

If the coating seems too thin, an extra coat can be given between the lines especially over the larger areas. This must be done before the baking. A pipette may be used for putting on this coat. This deepening has the bad effect of increasing the chance of the coating stripping from the metal.

The matrix thus prepared is used in the press just as is the ordinary plaster matrix. It is suited for reproduction of autographs, scrip, diagrams, etc.

CHAPTER IX.

THE MAKING OF VARIOUS SMALL ARTICLES OF INDIA RUBBER.

INDIA rubber can be so readily shaped in moulds and the latter are so readily made of plaster of paris that any one who is interested in such things will find endless amusement in working out different designs. Before suggesting any specific articles the following are the general points to be kept in mind.

The material may be uncured mixed sheet of any thickness. As we have seen this material when heated and pressed runs together. It can be forced into any shape by comparatively slight pressure. So exactly does it reproduce the smallest line or mark, that care must be taken to have the moulds very smooth and free from defect. Powdered soapstone is used to prevent adherence to the mould, but great care must be taken not to mix it among the pieces of the india rubber, where several are used in one article, as it will prevent their coalescing or running together.

Another point is to contrive to introduce the proper quantity of rubber. The aim must be to have a slight excess, but to avoid waste this should be as little as possible. Unless some rubber is squeezed out there is no certainty that the mould has been filled. Any projecting "fins" from the overflow are cut off with a knife or scissors after the article is removed from the mould.

Plaster of paris or dental plaster mixed with dextrine or gum arabic water or the zinc oxychloride cement, already described, is to be recommended for the moulds. They should be made, if deep, in frames or "flasks" of tin, as plaster if unsupported is liable to split open when the rubber is forced home.

For many articles the hot press can be used. Such articles are mats and other thin flat pieces. The rubber stamp sheet is a good material for them. For thicker articles a thicker sheet can be used, and sheet of any gauge can be procured from the maker. Much of what has been said about india rubber type applies to the making of miscellaneous shapes. It will also be understood where wooden moulds are spoken of that plaster, or, still better, metal can be substituted, and is to be recommended for nice work as the grain of the wood is very apt to show where the india rubber comes in contact with it.

Suction discs and similar small articles into which an extra thickness of india rubber enters are best cured in a vulcanizer. The flower pot arrangement is excellent for such. The time for curing may be somewhat extended on account of the greater thickness of material to be acted on.

Suction Discs.—For suction discs a mould is required which will produce a shallow cup with the edge feathered or reduced to a very slight thickness. Its outer surface should be raised in the centre so as to give a projection for attachment of the hook. The discs are generally made small, not over an inch in diameter, as they are not reliable for any heavy service. Their principal use is to suspend advertising cards and light articles to the glass of show windows. The following is a method of making a simple mould.

A hole to give the outside contour should be bored in a small piece of wood. A marble which will exactly fit the hole is next required. Some plaster of paris is mixed with water and put into the bottom of the hole, and the oiled marble is pressed down until the plaster rises and fills the entire space under the marble. After it has set the marble is removed. The proportions should be so arranged that the plaster will have risen at the sides within an eighth of an inch of the surface of the wood. This gives the exterior mould. For the cup or hollow a marble a shade too large to enter the hole may be used.

One or if necessary two thicknesses of mixed sheet rubber cut into disc shape so as to fit the hole are inserted in the block, and the larger marble is placed on top and screwed down by the press. Heat is now applied in the vulcanizer. When the thermometer indicates 212° F. (100° C.), or better a little more, the mould is withdrawn and the screws turned until the rubber is forced down and the excess begins to squeeze out between the marble and the wood, which two should now nearly touch. It is replaced and the heat is brought up to the curing temperature 284° F. (140° C.). It is possible that a second screwing up may be needed. The spring press is in such cases particularly convenient as it avoids the necessity for removing the press from the vulcanizing chamber. After half an hour it will be thoroughly cured. A hole is made through its centre from side to side thereof, but not penetrating the disc, and through this hole a brass nail is thrust and bent into hook form.

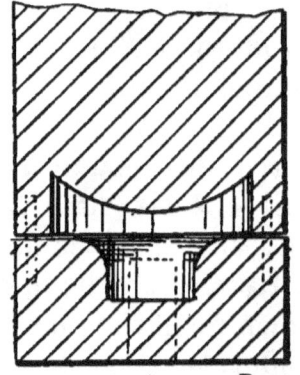

Mould for Suction Discs.

In the cut the correct shape for the mould and consequently for a suction disc is shown. This can be easily secured where a disc already made is procurable by casting in plaster, or, with a little ingenuity the template for the mould and the plunger to be used instead of the marble can be whittled out of wood. The lower body of the mould in such a case can be made of plaster of paris. To secure the alignment of the two parts of the mould, dowel pins, indicated in dotted lines, should be placed near the periphery. The gum should be introduced in a **lump** near the centre, in order that it may sink well downwards to the bottom of the mould before spreading laterally. Sometimes the tips have a recessed end. This is secured by the use of a mandrel, shown in dotted lines in the axis of the mould. Such discs are sometimes made to be cemented to arrows to be discharged against smooth surfaced targets, to which they adhere on impact by atmospheric pressure, giving rise to a very interesting game.

Another use of suction discs is as photographic negative holders. They can be fastened to a wooden handle and be attached by suction to the back of a negative under treatment. For this purpose they should be at least two inches in diameter.

Pencil Tips.—These are generally little cylinders of india rubber, which fit into a tube that slides over the end of the pencil. They can be thus simply made. A hole is bored in a piece of wood the diameter of and a little more than the depth of the pencil tip. A short cylinder that exactly fits the hole is required for plunger. The gum is put into the hole in little discs, or rolled up into a cylinder, the plunger is placed on top, and the mould put in the press. It is shaped by pressure and cured as described.

Sometimes the tips are cup shaped. For these the mould is made in two sections fastened by catches or by pins set in the plaster as shown in the cut. The hole is made larger at bottom than at top, and at the top is a little smaller than the shaft of the pencil. A plunger that nearly fits the small end is provided. The india rubber is placed in the mould and heated. When soft, the plunger is forced down to the proper distance in the press and the article is cured. Care must be taken to

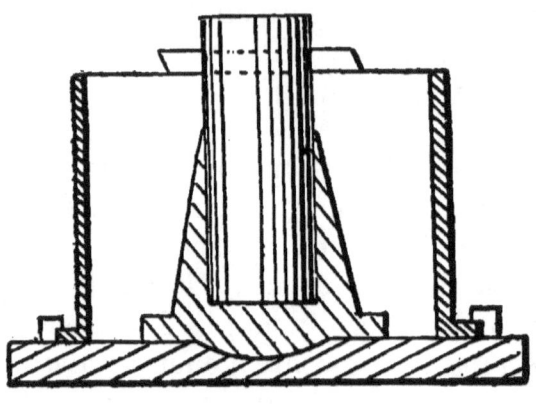

MOULD FOR PENCIL TIPS.

give the plunger a good coating of talc, and it must be made to sit vertically. The arrangement of a cylindrical hole shown in the cut secures this result perfectly. As distance piece a pin is passed through the plunger.

Cane and Chair Leg Tips, etc.—By carrying out the process just described with larger moulds and of slightly different section very convenient tips for chair legs and walking canes can be made. Such tips can be modified in size and thickness to answer as covers for the mouths of bottles, test-tubes, etc.

Corks.—These may be made in moulds tapering

from top to bottom. The india rubber must be packed in with great care to secure as solid filling as possible. A plunger is used that enters the larger end and is a very little smaller in diameter, so as to descend a little way into the mould. This distance determines the length of the cork. As the perimeter of the plunger strikes the walls of the mould it cuts off almost completely the excess of rubber

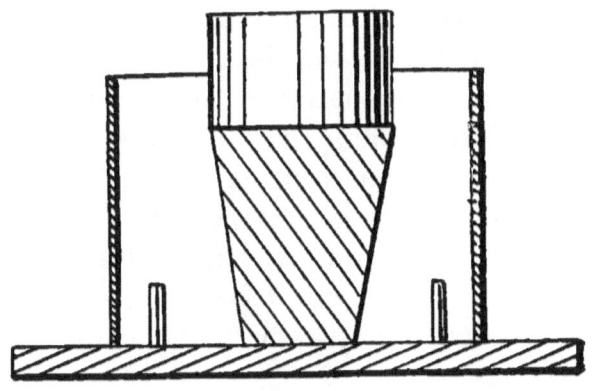

MOULD FOR RUBBER CORKS.

that has squeezed up past it. An excellent modification of the mould is shown in the cut. The upper part with parallel sides serves as a guide for the plunger. It is a similar extension as the one recommended to be used for the plunger in the hollow pencil and chair leg tip moulds just spoken of.

Mats.—These may generally be made in the hot press. Designs for them in great variety may be found in cut glass and pressed glass dishes. Many of these have patterns on their bottoms that can be moulded in plaster to serve as matrices.

Cord, Thread and Seamless Tube.—By placing the mixed india rubber in a cylindrical mould fitted with piston and with one or more round holes in the bottom, the material may be softened by heat and forced out of the holes by depressing the piston. This will form cylindrical thread or cord. As it descends it may be received in a box of powdered talc and be afterwards cured. By providing the hole with a mandrel seamless tubing may be thus made. In making such the mandrel usually remains in place during the curing. Plenty of powdered talc must be used.

Skeletonized Leaves as Models.—These would form interesting models from which matrices could be made in plaster. It would be possible to produce some very pretty stamps or mats from these and similar models.

After some experience inspection of any article will show how it was moulded. The fin will indicate the joint in the mould, and with this as a clew the mould can be almost certainly constructed like the original.

India Rubber Bulbs.—Bulbs and hollow articles generally, such as dolls, toys and the like, cannot be made without special high pressure hollow moulds. The general process consists in cutting out gores from mixed sheet as for a balloon. The edges are coated with cement (thick benzole or carbon disulphide india rubber solution) and while the rubber is warm the seams are pressed and knitted together with the fingers. A hole is left in one place through which some pure water or water of ammonia is introduced. The bulb is now blown up with the mouth or otherwise, and while inflated the hole is pressed shut. This is often done with the teeth. Any projections around the seams are cut off with curved scissors. The mould is of iron and in two halves. Powdered talc is applied, and the bulb is placed in and shut up in the mould which it should exactly fill. The mould is clamped together and the whole is put into a vulcanizer, and the rubber is cured. The steam and vapor formed by its liquid contents expand it and press it with great force against the sides of the mould. After curing the mould and bulb are removed from the vulcanizer, cooled by a shower bath of cold water, the mould is opened and the bulb is removed. Often an iron pin is left projecting through the side during the vulcanizing, which pin, when withdrawn, leaves the necessary aperture, or it is perforated. The bulbs are polished by tumbling in a revolving cylinder. Considerable skill and practice are needed to succeed in making hollow bulbs. Great accuracy is needed in cutting out the gores and in joining the seams.

CHAPTER X.

THE MANIPULATION OF MASTICATED SHEET RUBBER.

The manipulation of pure sheet rubber is simple, yet is liable to lead to disappointment. When two pieces are laid face to face and cut across with a sharp knife, or scissors, the edges will adhere with considerable tenacity. This may be increased by applying some thick solution of india rubber in a volatile solvent, and by manipulating the sheets so as to bring the entire surfaces of the cuts together. Finally the material may be charged with sulphur by absorption or by Parkes' process, and cured in a glycerine or calcium chloride bath, all of which are described in chapter XI. The same treatment will affect the cement used in making the joint also, bringing about its vulcanization.

Such in a few words is the main process in the treatment of this class of goods. Where it is desired to prevent adherence, soapy water or powdered talc is used.

Adherence may be produced between the surfaces of the sheets if they are clean, by pressure and a little warmth. The method of making toy balloons will give an example of how the article is dealt with by the manufacturer.

A pile of pieces of masticated sheet rubber is made. Every piece has one side coated with powdered talc, and two talc-coated sides are placed in contact in each pair. As they are piled up, the outer surfaces of each pair are moistened with water. A steel punch or die, pear shaped in outline, is used to cut down through the pile, cutting all the pieces into that shape.

The pile is then taken apart in pairs. The separation takes place between the wet surfaces, the edges of each pair adhering slightly so as to enclose the talc-coated surfaces. The neck is opened if necessary. A rather weak or thin solution of india rubber in benzole is now brushed over the freshly cut edges. By pulling out the centre of each piece the edges are brought into contact, and adherence is produced.

If the Parkes process of vulcanizing, chapter XI., is employed they are cured to the slight extent necessary upon a tray coated with talc. The balloons are then ready for inflation.

They are rather delicate articles to make except for immediate use as the thin material is liable to become over vulcanized.

In the chemical laboratory sheet rubber can be used for covering the ends of glass stirring rods. These answer very nicely for cleaning out from beakers the last particles of a precipitate. The sheet is cut of proper size and is bent around the end of the rod and cut off close with a pair of scissors. It adheres where cut. It is then pinched with the fingers to bring the edges into better contact and the operation is complete. A slight heat makes it adhere better.

To connect glass tubes in setting up laboratory apparatus the same material was formerly used. It was wrapped around the joint, tied with thread and slightly warmed. At present this form of connection is wholly displaced by ready made rubber tubing.

It is interesting to observe in all articles made from this sheet the marks of the original cutting knife. These may be observed in inflated balloons, as parallel lines running all over the surface, and magnified by the expansion due to the inflation.

CHAPTER XI.

VARIOUS VULCANIZING AND CURING METHODS.

The regular methods of vulcanizing and curing can be departed from and good results obtained. A few excellent methods differing essentially from the ordinary ones are described which will be of service to workers on the small scale, as they enable one to dispense with vulcanizer and air bath entirely.

One type of curing process does away with the air or steam vulcanizer, and substitutes, as the curing agency, a hot bath of liquid. For this purpose a fluid is required that will not act injuriously upon the india rubber, and which will give a curing temperature without boiling away. One favorite liquid is glycerine. This can be heated to the necessary degree and is an excellent substitute for the expensive apparatus often used. For experimental work it is exceedingly convenient.

In use it is placed in a vessel of proper size and a thermometer is suspended so that its bulb dips into the liquid near one side and does not touch the bottom of the vessel. The heat is applied by a gas burner, alcohol lamp or oil stove. Of course the vessel may be placed on an ordinary cooking stove or range, and the heat may be graduated and adjusted by moving it about until it reaches a part of the stove where the proper heat will be maintained.

The mould with its contents is immersed in the glycerine, care being taken to see that it so placed as to assume the mean temperature of the liquid and not to be heated too hot. This might happen if it stood on the bottom of the vessel, so it is well to have it supported or suspended a little above it.

It is easy to see that the whole may be so arranged that the screw handle or pressure nuts of the mould will rise above the liquid. In this case the press can be screwed down while the article is heating.

Instead of glycerine a strong solution of some salt in water has been recommended. A solution of calcium chloride, or some other salt can be substituted. Either are very cheap and will be quite satisfactory.

Another treatment which applies also to the mixing operation is by the sulphur bath. Sulphur is melted in an iron vessel and brought to a temperature of 248° F. (120° C.). A piece of unmixed pure caoutchouc immersed in this bath will gradually absorb sulphur. The case is almost parallel with the absorption of water or benzole by the gum. The piece swells and thickens as it is acted on and eventually will contain enough sulphur for vulcanization. It may absorb as much as fifty per cent. The point of proper absorption must be settled more or less empirically or by successive trials.

After enough has been taken up the piece is removed and dipped into cold water, which cracks the adherent sulphur so that it can be brushed or rubbed off. This gives a piece of mixed rubber ready for moulding and curing. It can be heated and moulded and may be cured as desired, in a liquid bath, hot press or vulcanizer.

It will be observed that this provides for the admixture of sulphur only; no talc or other solid can be thus introduced. The addition of these solids tends to make the rubber of a more attractive color and their use is not to be deprecated in all cases. Hence the sulphur bath process is not to be considered a perfect one.

In the sulphur bath the mixing and curing processes can be combined. If the liquid sulphur is heated to the vulcanizing temperature, 284° F. (140° C.), a thin strip of gum immersed in it will be vulcanized completely in a few minutes. A heating of several hours at the lower temperature will effect the same result.

The sulphur bath processes must be regarded as unsatisfactory. It is not easy to feel that any dependence can be placed upon them as regards reliability or constancy of product. The sulphur also will mostly effect the surface. Thin pieces may be satisfactorily treated, but the same confidence cannot be felt as is experienced when specific amounts of ingredients have been mixed in with pure caoutchouc in a regular mixing machine.

The sulphur bath is of value to the experimenter, enabling him to do his own mixing without expensive apparatus.

Bromine, iodine, chlorine and nitric acid are vulcanizers. A piece of sheet rubber dipped into liquid bromine is instantly vulcanized. Iodine and nitric acid have also been used in commercial work.

Alkaline or alkaline earth sulphides can be employed in solution under pressure for vulcanizing. At a vulcanizing temperature their solutions will answer for thin sheet very well. Polysulphides of calcium have thus been employed.

By simply lying embedded in finely divided sulphur at a temperature of 233° F. (112° C.) as much as ten per cent. of sulphur may be absorbed by thin sheet rubber. This is one of the processes peculliarly suited for work on the small scale. It may be used instead of the Parkes process next to be described.

Chloride of sulphur is an orange red mobile liquid of a peculiar and disagreeable odor. It boils at 276° F. (136° C.). It dissolves both sulphur and chlorine so that it is not easy to obtain it in a pure state. If unmixed india rubber is exposed to its action it will quickly become vulcanized. At ordinary temperatures the mixing action takes place, though it is much accelerated by a slight application of heat.

It is quite possible that this action may be of use to the reader in his manipulation of india rubber. Thin sheet may be vulcanized by being immersed in a solution of this substance in bisulphide of carbon followed by slight heating. The thin layer of caoutchouc left by evaporation of the chloroform solution of india rubber may thus be vulcanized so as to become comparatively strong and elastic. Where the same solution has been used as a cement or for patching overshoes and finishing the patch, a vulcanization can thus be given to it.

The process is known as Parkes' cold curing process.

A solution of one part of chloride of sulphur in forty parts of bisulphide of carbon is of good strength for rapid work. A thin article needs but an instant of immersion. It then is placed in a box or tray upon some talc powder and is heated to about 104° F., (40° C.). One minute of curing will suffice. It is advisable to wash off the articles afterwards in water or in weak lye to remove any traces of acid.

Petroleum naptha can be used as the solvent instead of bisulphide of carbon. The latter substance has an exceedingly disagreeable odor, and its vapors must be considered rather injurious especially to those who are not accustomed to them.

When thick articles are to be cured by this process a much more diluted solution is used. One per cent. or less of the chloride of sulphur is the proportion used. The object of this is to enable a longer immersion to be employed so that the interior will be affected before the outer layers become too much charged with the vulcanizing material.

In this short description of the Parkes curing process hints for a useful method may be found. The process is beyond doubt by far the simplest known for treatment of india rubber. Exactly what reaction takes place is unknown. Whether the sulphur or the chlorine is the acting vulcanizer has not as yet been determined.

Its defect is that it produces surface action, analogous to casehardening. One method of avoiding this is to remove the articles from the sulphur chloride bath and at once to immerse them in water. This prevents the rapid volatilization of the solvent and an equalizing of the absorption ensues.

CHAPTER XII.

THE SOLUTION OF INDIA RUBBER.

India rubber presents some difficulties in its solution. If a piece of pure gum just as received by the factory is placed in hot water it will swell and whiten after a while, but will not dissolve. If a similar piece is placed in benzole a similar but greatly exaggerated action takes place. The piece if left to soak for a day or more swells enormously, but very little solution is effected.

The swollen india rubber can be removed from the benzole in a single piece. It will display all the layers and marks of the original piece which was perhaps of not one hundredth part of its volume. Some parts will be a perfect transparent jelly.

It has been found that masticated india rubber dissolves with comparatively little difficulty. If the experimenter will place in a porcelain mortar, the jelly-like mass obtained as above detailed, and will rub it up thoroughly, it will be effectually masticated. This requires a little patience, as the slippery material seems to elude the pestle. Yet eventually it will all be reduced to a perfectly homogeneous mass. Its action while being rubbed up is very peculiar. At first no progress seems to be made. After a little the lumps yield to the friction. The rubber then begins to attach itself to the pestle and mortar, and begins to be drawn out into ever changing webs and threads. As the operation approaches completion the material makes a snapping, crackling noise familiar to all rubber workers. When complete there will be no lump left, and the whole will be a uniform pulp.

If benzole or a volatile solvent has been used, the rubber will easily be removed from the mortar with a spatula or palette knife. If turpentine was the solvent it will be impossible to remove the last traces except after long standing or by solution.

If replaced in the original solvent it will now come into nearly or quite perfect solution. This is the best way of masticating on the small scale. It is almost impossible to masticate untreated gum in an ordinary mortar.

The dealers sell a special india rubber for the manufacture of cement and solutions. This is so treated by mastication that it dissolves with great readiness. It is also said that heating under pressure is used to dissolve it in some factories.

Many solvents have been used and none work without some difficulty. Benzole, coal tar naptha, petroleum naptha, carbon disulphide, ether and chloroform, oil of turpentine and caoutchoucin are the best known. The naptha best suited for its solution is termed solvent naptha. It has a specific gravity of .850 at 60° F. (15½° C.); it boils at from 240° F. (115½° C.) to 250° F. (121° C.) and on evaporation should leave no more than ten per cent. of residue at 320° F. (160° C.)

Payen recommends a mixture of 95 parts bisulphide of carbon with 5 parts of absolute alcohol.

Commercial chloroform is apt to be too impure to act as a good solvent. It is apt to contain alcohol mixed with it as a preservative, which impairs its effectiveness.

Some of these solutions are better suited than others for the deposition of thin layers by evaporation. Turpentine gives a very sticky and unmanageable solution, which dries very slowly. Payen's solution and the chloroform and the benzole solutions may be cited as especially adapted for this purpose. Careful vulcanization by the cold curing method can be applied to articles made by such deposition from evaporation.

In the case of all of them some form of mastication for the india rubber is needed. The simple mortar grinding of the gum swelled by the solvent is the only practical treatment without special apparatus.

When it is remembered that fixed oils are destroyers of vulcanized or unvulcanized india rubber it will be obvious how important it is to use pure solvents. Too great care cannot be taken to preserve the liquids pure and free from such matter.

A solid hydrocarbon may be used. Thus paraffin wax, such as candles are made of, when melted acts as a solvent. The resulting liquid solidifies when it cools, retaining an almost greasy feel.

Boiling oil of turpentine is recommended by some for the solution of vulcanized india rubber. Phenyle sulphide, it is stated, will soften it so as to render it workable. The latter discovery is credited to Dr. Stenhouse.

It is stated that a solution or pasty mixture of one part of caoutchouc in eleven parts of turpentine with one half part of a hot concentrated solution of sulphur (potassium sulphide) gives on evaporation a film neither tacky nor soft, a species of vulcanization taking place.

It is of much interest to note that an aqueous solution of india rubber has been proposed in which the vehicle is a solution of borax in water. This is well known to be a solvent for shellac and other resins. It has been recommended often as a vehicle for rubbing up india ink. The ink made by mixing lampblack with the shellac solution is nearly waterproof. A shellac varnish is given by the plain solution.

The experiments upon india rubber were published in a recent trade paper. One method of making the solution is as follows.

A solution of borax two fifths saturated is made by adding to two volumes of saturated solution three volumes of water. To this is added a solution of india rubber in benzole or other hydrocarbon of such strength and in such quantity as to contain from three and one-half to four and one-half per cent. of india rubber referred to the borax solution. It is now vigorously shaken and heated to 120°–140° F. (49°–60° C.) and the agitation, not too violent, is continued until it cools. Ceara or Madagascar rubber answers best; Para is not so good for this formula. This may be termed the indirect or emulsion method.

For direct solution from two to three volumes of water may be added to three volumes of saturated borax solution. The india rubber is added in extremely thin shavings and the solution is heated. For weak solutions the boiling point need not be reached. For strong solutions the heating should be done under pressure so as to bring up the pressure to one to three atmospheres.

Such solutions may contain as much as eight per cent. of the gum. The mixture is liable to coagulate or gelatinize just at the wrong time, but it may be of value as a vehicle or as a waterproofing agent. It deserves further investigation, which it is to be hoped it will duly receive.

Great care is necessary in working with naptha, benzole, carbon disulphide and similar liquids. Their vapor is given off at ordinary temperatures and may travel some distance to a lamp or fire and become ignited and carry the flame back to the vessel. Their vapors are also anæsthetic and should be avoided as regards inhalation.

CHAPTER XIII.

EBONITE, VULCANITE AND GUTTA-PERCHA.

Ebonite and Vulcanite.—These two well known substances are india rubber, in which the vulcanization process has been intensified. From twenty-five to fifty per cent. of sulphur is added in the mixing, and the curing is prolonged to several hours. A temperature of 275° F. (135° C.) for six to ten hours is sometimes recommended, but generally a shorter period at the regular temperature, 284° F. (140° C.), may be employed.

The mixed sheet is made and sold extensively for dentists' use. It is soft and flexible and very easily moulded. It is treated like the regular mixed sheet in every respect, except that plumbago brushed on the slightly oiled surface of the mould is recommended instead of the light colored talc, to prevent adherence. Wax where available is better than oil.

Sometimes specimens are built up in sections. About an hour before full vulcanization in the fourth stage, new material can be added and will attach itself to the old. The stages of vulcanization are thus given by Bolas.

"Several distinct stages or steps may be traced during the curing of ebonite; and I wish to call your attention to some specimens illustrating these various stages.

"Here, in the first place, is the plain mixture of sulphur and rubber, this being nearly white, and capable of becoming quite plastic or soft by the application of a gentle heat.

"The second specimen illustrates the action of a very moderate degree of heat on the mixed material, this particular sample having been heated to 128° Centigrade for twenty minutes. It is, as you see, somewhat darkened, and has lost a little of its original softness; while a degree of heat which would have rendered the original mixture plastic, like putty, fails to make much impression upon it.

"The third specimen illustrates the effect of a more prolonged heating, this sample having been heated for an hour to 135° Centigrade. It is olive green in color, and has acquired a certain amount of elasticity, resembling that of a rather inferior quality of vulcanized caoutchouc.

"The fourth stage of curing is illustrated by this specimen, which you see is brown, and tolerably hard. Ebonite in this state refuses altogether to become plastic by heat, and a temperature of 150° maintained for half an hour or less would suffice to bring it to the fifth stage, or that of finished ebonite.

"The fifth stage, or that of properly cured

ebonite, is the goal to be arrived at in manufacturing the material. There should be no places where the curing is imperfect, a kind of defect which is likely to happen when articles of unusual thickness are vulcanized, and no portion of the ebonite should be spongy or honeycombed by air bubbles.

"The sixth, or spongy state, is generally the result of over-heating, bubbles of gas forming in the material, and converting it into a kind of porous, cinder-like mass.

"A specimen will now be handed round, which illustrates the third, fourth, fifth and sixth stages, as already described. The specimen in question was cured on a hot plate, this having probably been heated to 160° or 170° Centigrade; and you will be able to trace all gradations in the curing operation, from the first setting of the plastic material to the destruction of the ebonite by overheating."

Cement for uniting pieces of the partially cured material may be made by rubbing up some of the untreated scrap with benzole.

At the heat of boiling water, ebonite can be bent to a certain extent, which bend it retains on cooling. When warm an impression of a coin or relief die may be made on it by heavy pressure which it will retain. On heating the image disappears. If before heating the surface is planed off and the piece is heated the image formerly in intaglio will expand into relief.

By the exact process of rubber stamp making

excellent stereotype plates may be made of ebonite.

It can be turned at high speed in a lathe and polished with fine 000 emery paper followed by a cloth bob with rotten stone, etc., and water or oil. Blotting paper, charged with the above or with tripoli, is excellent for polishing small surfaces by hand.

Ebonite is a good connecting material between softer rubber and iron, the whole being vulcanized together; the iron should be well roughened or cut into rasp-like or file-like projections.

Ebonite is properly the name for black hard rubber, and vulcanite for the colored products such as used by dentists and others.

GUTTA-PERCHA.

Gutta-percha is prepared by coagulation from the juice or sap of several trees, among others the *Isonandra gutta*, of Borneo and the East Indian Archipelago. The product gutta-percha is identical in composition with india rubber. It is hard at all ordinary temperatures.

Its manufacture includes purification and mastication. It is far more amenable to treatment than is india rubber. Many materials are mixed with it as adulterants or otherwise in the factories.

It is more useful in the form of sheets. These when heated to 122° F. (50° C.) become pliable and can be moulded by pressure to any degree. At the temperature of boiling water it becomes pasty and adhesive, and at 266° F. (130° C.) it is so soft that it may be considered as melted.

It is an admirable moulding material. Stereotypes and other relief or intaglio images can be made by pressing it while heated. These are often absolutely perfect reproductions of the original.

Dishes for photographic purposes, etc., are easily made out of the sheet. By gentle warming they become pliable, and a greater heat makes surfaces capable of adhering by pressure.

Tubes can be made by the squirting process, as used for india rubber. Wires are coated with it in a similar manner.

It has several defects. It is not durable if exposed to the air with consequent changes of temperature. It is also too easily softened by heat, as of course no hot liquid can be introduced into a guttapercha vessel. The Parkes cold curing process can be applied to it, which makes it more indifferent to heat. This is applied by dipping an instant and drying. After several repetitions the period of dipping is prolonged and ultimately it is left immersed some time. If left immersed at first it would dissolve.

It is soluble in most caoutchouc solvents, particularly in carbon disulphide.

CHAPTER XIV.

GLUE OR COMPOSITION STAMPS.

Stamps made from a mixture of glue, glycerine, and molasses or from similar mixtures are an excellent substitute for india rubber stamps. Properly made they possess all the flexibility that characterizes the rubber ones, while for fatty inks such as that used by printers and lithographers, which inks tend to destroy rubber stamps, they are much better. They are adopted by the United States government for making dating stamps for use in the Post Office Department; by publishers of directories for printing advertisements on the edges of their publications, and in many other cases. Our description shall follow as closely as possible the process and methods used in the United States Post Office. They are there termed "composition blotters."

The composition of which they are made is printer's roller material. Nine and one-half pounds of fine quality glue are soaked in just enough soft water to cover it until it is thoroughly softened. It is then melted. In the Government Department a steam kettle is provided for the purpose. An ordinary glue pot will answer for smaller quantities.

When melted four and one-half pounds of best molasses and seven pounds of glycerine are added, and the whole is thoroughly mixed. The formula varies a little according to the prevailing temperature, less molasses being added when the weather is warm, and *vice versa*. Experience is here the best teacher. When well mixed it is poured out into tin pails whose inner walls or sides and bottom have been

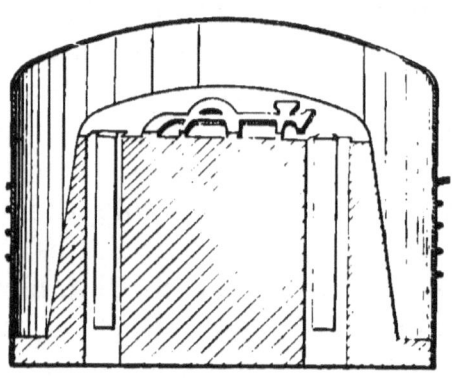

MODEL FOR COMPOSITION STAMP MOULD.

rubbed over with oil. It solidifies in cooling and becomes a clear brown jelly quite free from any stickiness or superficial moistness.

In use it is turned out of the pails to which, owing to the oiling, it does not adhere. It is cut off as wanted, melted by heat and cast in oiled moulds.

The latter are made of type metal to which one-third its weight of lead has been added. As model for the mould or matrix a brass model of the stamp is employed. This represents a sort of oval based cut-off or truncated cone, about an inch high and a little over an inch long on its base. A flange extends outward from its base and a tube is provided to fit this flange. Its smaller end corresponds to the face of the stamp, and on it are engraved in full relief any permanent characters,

COMPOSITION STAMP MOULD.

circles or border lines, etc. Through its centre one or more apertures are made. Into these, changeable steel, iron or brass type may be introduced and set fast with plaster of paris.

To make the mould, the brass model with its movable type set as required is placed upon a flat table or plate, face upward, and surrounded by the tube, as shown in partial section in the cut, page 114. The tube is a strip of sheet iron, which is bent around the flange and is secured in place by a wire twisted around it. The melted alloy (type, metal and lead) is poured into the space thus formed until it rises a quarter of an inch above the face of the model. In a few minutes it sets and is removed and allowed to cool. This gives a cup with the inscription and design depressed or in *intaglio* upon its inside base. This is shown in the cut, page 115, partly in section; it will of course be understood that the mould forms a complete cup.

To make the stamp the interior surface of the mould is oiled with a stiff brush. It is not material what oil is used. The composition melted by heat is then poured into the cup, and is allowed to solidify. Owing to the conical shape of the mould it is readily removed. The mould must be hot but not too much so.

In the Post Office stamps the date requires to be changed frequently. Some of the figures do duty for two or three days each month. Thus the figure 8 is in the designation of three days, the eighth, eighteenth, and twenty-eighth. There are three changes involved therefore in connection with this day numeral. When a stamp mould or matrix is cast the place of numerals that are to be changed is filled with a blank space in the part where the type would otherwise come. A number is stamped in this space when needed, by means of an ordinary steel number-punch.

When the number is to be changed the old character is scraped or cut out, leaving a small irregular hollow. A very small piece of soft lead, about one-sixteenth of an inch on each side, is dropped into the hollow. With a flat faced punch it is flattened out, and on it the new number is impressed by a steel punch. This operation is repeated a great many times before the matrix is worn out.

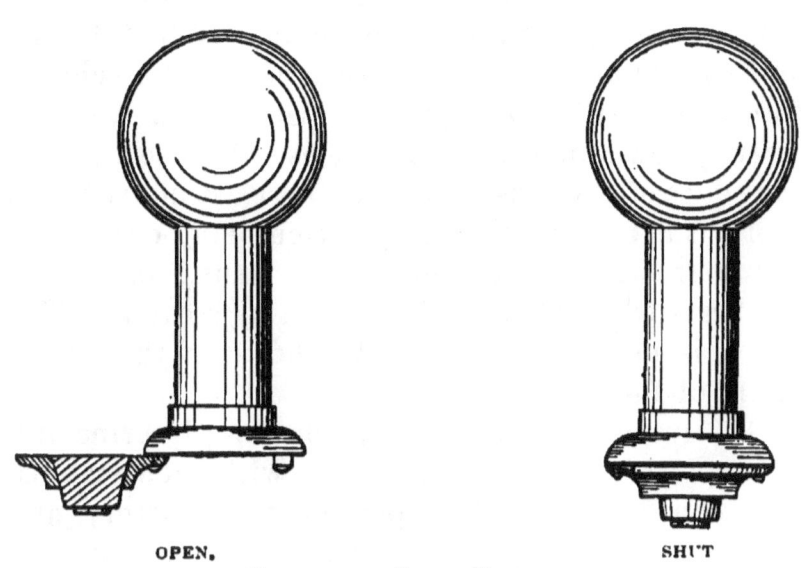

OPEN.   SHUT.
COMPOSITION STAMP HANDLE.

In the cut, page 115, one number is shown as stamped into the soft lead, and at the other end of the stamp is a blank space ready for a number.

The casting of a stamp is so extremely simple that no attempt is made to use movable type, as in permanent rubber dating stamps.

While it is obvious that these composition stamps could be attached directly to wooden handles, a special style of handle, shown in the cuts, is employed by the Post Office. A wooden handle carries at its end a brass base, to which is pivoted a swinging piece that is perforated by a conical oval aperture a little larger than the small end of the stamp. The edges of this aperture are slightly rounded.

It is swung around as shown in the first figure, and the stamp, previously moistened on its sides, is forced in. If the stamp is properly made it is surprising how much force may be used to insert it. If the edges of the brass swinging piece are not rounded there is danger of the composition being cut. The stamp in its brass frame is then swung back over the brass base, where it is secured by a catch. The stamp is now ready for use, as shown in the second figure of the cut.

It is imperative that no aqueous or glycerine ink be employed for continuous work with such stamps. Common printers' ink is perfectly satisfactory, and the work may be nearly or quite as good as that executed by an india rubber stamp.

The Post Office manufactures a pad for use with printers' ink into whose manufacture the same composition enters. The ink retainer is a piece of fine felt, one-quarter to one-half an inch thick. This is placed in the bottom of a shallow steel mould, where it enters for half its depth into a recess that it accurately fits. The composition from old stamps, melted up, is then poured upon and around it, the mould being previously oiled. When it is full a piece of strong manilla paper, of the area of the felt only, is placed upon the bottom of the glue pad on its centre, which as it lies in the mould is its uppermost part. The paper adheres strongly as the glue hardens. Eventually it is turned out of the mould, and a pad, shown in the cut, is produced. The dotted lines show the limits of the felt pad. The glue composition underlies, surrounds and extends outwards from the felt portion. It is found that the elasticity of the composition makes the pad

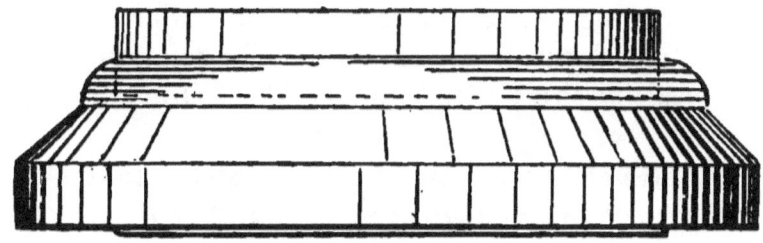

Composition Ink Pad.

much pleasanter for rapid stamping.

The above description gives the clew to making any stamp of this description. The matrix may be of dental plaster, or of oxychloride of zinc cement. The mould may be built up of type of any kind.

The composition is so cheap that the stamp can be made quite thick. This gives it a high degree of elasticity and adaptability to uneven surfaces. It may be mounted by adherence upon a flat board or block, provided, if necessary, with handles. If the board or block is placed upon the composition while it is still warm and liquid, as it solidifies the board and composition will adhere with great tenacity.

All moulds or surfaces to which it is desired that the melted composition shall not adhere must be oiled.

The moulds must not be cold or the composition will not enter the fine divisions. If on the other hand they are too hot the mixture will adhere. Experience will teach the right conditions for success.

Below are given other formulæ for roller composition. The formula already given in this chapter is that used by the United States Post Office Department.

I. "Old Home Receipt:" Glue 2 lbs., soaked over night, to New Orleans molasses 1 gallon. Not durable, but excellent while it lasts.

II. Glue 10½ lbs., molasses 2½ gal., Venice turpentine 2 oz., glycerine 12 oz.; mix as directed above.

CHAPTER XV.

THE HEKTOGRAPH.

For obtaining multiple copies of writing, the apparatus called the Hektograph or Papyrograph has been extensively adopted. In general terms it consists of a tray filled with a jelly like composition. Any imprint made upon the surface with aniline ink can be transferred to paper by simple pressure. The tray filled with composition is called the tablet. It is thus prepared.

The tray may be made of tin or even of pasteboard or paper, and should be about one half an inch deep. It may be of any size, according to the work it is to do. The composition is made from the best gelatine and glycerine. One ounce by weight of gelatine is soaked over night in cold water, and in the morning the water is poured off, leaving the swelled gelatine. Six and one-half fluid ounces of glycerine are now heated to about 200 F. (93 C.) on a water bath preferably, and the gelatine is added thereto. The heating is continued for several hours. This operates to expel the water and to give a clear glycerine solution of gelatine.

The composition is then poured into the tray,

which must be perfectly level in order to obtain a a surface nearly even with the edge. It is then covered so as to keep off the dust. The cover of course must not come in contact with the smooth surface. In six hours it will be ready for use.

The original copy that is to be reproduced is made upon ordinary paper in aniline ink. One formula for the ink reads as follows: Aniline violet or blue (2 R B or 3 B) 1 oz., hot water 7 fluid oz.; dissolve. After cooling add alcohol 1 fluid oz. and glycerine ¼ fluid oz., a few drops of ether and a drop of carbolic acid. Keep in a corked bottle. Other formulæ are given in chapter XVII.

The writing is executed with an ordinary steel pen. The lines should be rather heavy so as to show a greenish color by reflected light.

The surface of the pad is slightly moistened with a wet sponge and is allowed to become nearly dry. The paper is then laid upon it and smoothed down. This is best done by placing a second sheet over it and rubbing this with the hand. No air bubbles must remain between the copy and the tablet, and the paper must not be shifted.

It is allowed to remain for a minute or less and is then raised by one corner and stripped from the gelatine surface. It will have left the reversed copy of its inscription perfectly reproduced upon the tablet.

At once a piece of ordinary writing paper of the desired size and quality is laid upon the tablet, smoothed down, and stripped off, when it will be found to have taken with it a complete copy of the inscription or writing. This is repeated over

THE HEKTOGRAPH.

and over again with another sheet of paper, until the ink on the pad is exhausted. Fifty or more good copies can be thus obtained.

As soon as the work is completed the remains of the ink should be washed off with a moist sponge and the tablet, after drying a little, will be ready for a second operation.

Some practice is required to ascertain the proper strength of the writing and degree of wetness of the surface. When the gelatine surface becomes impaired it can be remelted in a water bath if it is not too dark from absorption of ink.

French Ministery of Public Work Formula.—Glue 100 parts, glycerine 500 parts, finally powdered kaolin or barium sulphate 25 parts, water 375 parts. Use a little hydrochloric acid in the water for washing off the pad after use.

Hektograph Sheets.—Four parts of glue are soaked in five parts of water and three parts of ammonia until soft. It is then heated and there is added to it three parts of sugar and eight parts of glycerine. The mixture is applied to blotting paper. This is saturated with it, and successive coats added until a smooth surface is produced on one side. This is the side for reproduction. It is used like the regular tablet except that it is claimed that sponging off the writing is not necessary. Owing to the capillary action developed by the blotting paper it is supposed to be self-cleaning by standing.

CHAPTER XVI.

CEMENTS.

BEFORE cementing vulcanized rubber the surface should be roughened or still better it may be seared with a red hot iron. For bicycle tyres this is especially to be recommended.

Cement for Cuts in Bicycle Tyres, Rubber Belts, etc.—Carbon bisulphide, 5 ounces; gutta-percha, 5 ounces; caoutchouc, 10 ounces; fish glue, 2½ ounces. After it is applied and has dried the excess can be removed with a wet knife. Bad cuts should first be stitched up.

Bicycle Tyre Cement to fasten Tyres to Rims.—Equal parts of pitch and gutta-percha are melted together. Sometimes two parts of pitch are prescribed. This cement has extended application.

Cement for Paper Boats and for Mending Rubber Goods.—Fuse together equal parts of pitch and gutta-percha, and to this add about 2 parts of linseed oil containing 5 parts of litharge. Continue the heat until the ingredients are uniformly commingled. Apply warm.

Waterproof Cement.—Shellac, 4 oz; borax, 1 oz;

boil in a little water until dissolved, and concentrate by heat to a paste.

Another.—10 parts of carbon disulphide and **one** part of oil of turpentine are mixed, and as much gutta-percha is added as will readily dissolve.

Cement for Mending Hard Rubber.—Fuse together equal parts of gutta-percha and genuine asphaltum; apply hot to the joint, closing the latter immediately with pressure.

Glue to Fasten Leather, etc., to Metals.—1 part crushed nut galls digested 6 hours with 8 parts distilled water and strained. Glue is macerated in its own weight of water for 24 hours, and then dissolved. The warm infusion of nutgalls is spread on the leather; the glue solution upon the roughened surface of the warm metal; the moist leather is then pressed upon it and dried.

Marine Glue, Various Formulæ.—I. Dissolve 1 part of india rubber in 12 parts of benzole, and to the solution add 20 parts of powdered shellac, heating the mixture cautiously over a fire. There is great danger of conflagration. Apply with a brush.

II. Caoutchouc, 1 oz; genuine asphaltum, 2 oz; benzole or naptha, q. s. The caoutchouc is first dissolved (as described in chapter XII.), and the asphaltum is gradually added. The solution should have about the consistency of molasses.

Cement for Vulcanized India Rubber.—Stockholm pitch, 3 parts; American resin, 3 parts; unmixed india rubber, 6 parts; oil of turpentine, 12 parts.

Heat and mix very thoroughly. More oil of turpentine may be added as required.

Gutta-Percha Cement for Leather.—Soak gutta-percha in boiling water. Soften in benzole after cutting up for a day. Heat on a water bath until the greater part of the benzole is expelled. When cool it will solidify. Use by heating.

Cement for Rubber Shoes.—

(1) Chloroform .... 280 parts.
    India rubber (masticated) .... 10 "
(2) India rubber .... 10 "
    Resin .... 4 "
    Venice turpentine .... 2 "
    Oil of turpentine .... 40 "

For first solution dissolve by mastication. For second, melt the finely divided gum with the resin, add the Venice turpentine and finally the oil of turpentine. Use heat if necessary. Mix both solutions finally. To apply, saturate a piece of linen with the cement and apply to the spot previously coated with the cement. As it dries apply a little more as required. A finishing varnish is given in the last chapter. Parkes' cold curing process may be applied as described in chapter XI.

Chatterton's Compound for uniting sheets of gutta-percha in cable cores and for general work with gutta-percha coated wires.—Stockholm tar, 1 part; resin, 1 part; gutta-percha, 2 parts.

Waterproofing for Wooden Battery Cells.—Resin, 4 parts; gutta-percha, 1 part; boiled oil, a little.

Another Formula.—Burgundy pitch, 150 parts; old gutta-percha in fine shreds, 25 parts; ground pumice stone, 75 parts. Melt the gutta-percha and mix with the pumice stone and then add the pitch, melting all together. Apply melted and smooth off with a hot iron.

Cement for Celluloid.—Shellac, 1 part is dissolved in spirits of camphor 1 part, with 3 to 4 parts strong alcohol. It is applied warm and the parts united must not be disturbed until the cement is hard.

CHAPTER XVII.

INKS.

RUBBER STAMP INK.

Aniline blue soluble, 1 B.............	3	parts.
Distilled water.....................	10	"
Acetic acid........................	10	"
Alcohol...........................	10	"
Glycerine.........................	70	"

For other colors the following aniline colors may be substituted in proportions given:

Methyl violet, 3 B (violet)............	3	parts.
Diamond fuchsin I, (red).............	2	"
Methyl green yellowish...............	4	"
Vesuvin, B (brown)..................	5	"
Nigrosin, W (blue black).............	4	"

For very bright red 3 parts of Eosin BBN. are used. In this case the acetic acid must be omitted. In all cases the colors should first be rubbed up with the water in a mortar, and the glycerine should be added gradually. These inks will answer for the hektograph.

Hektograph Ink.—Aniline color, 1 part; water, 7 parts; glycerine, 1 part. A little alcohol may be used with advantage to dissolve the aniline color. It can be expelled by heating if it proves objectionable.

Aniline Ink Vehicle.—Prof. E. B. Shuttleworth, of Toronto, Ont., suggests the use of castor oil in place of vaseline and other vehicles for typewriter ink. The aniline colors may first be dissolved in alcohol, and the solution may be added to the oil. They may also be dissolved directly in the oil in which most of them are soluble.

Indelible Stamping Inks.—I. Asphaltum, 1 part; oil of turpentine, 4 parts; dissolve and temper with printer's ink. The ink may be omitted, and solid dry color added.

II. Sodium carbonate, 22 parts; glycerine, 85 parts; dissolve and rub up in a mortar with gum arabic, 20 parts. In a separate vessel dissolve silver nitrate, 11 parts; in officinal aqua ammonia, 20 parts. Mix the two solutions, and heat to the boiling point, 212° F. (100 C.). After it darkens, add Venice turpentine, 10 parts. After applying to the cloth, a hot iron should be applied, or it should be exposed to the sun.

III. Dr. W. Reissig's formula:

Boiled linseed oil varnish	16 parts.
Finest lamp black	6 "
Ferric chloride (sesquichloride of iron)	2 to 5 "

Dilute a little for use with varnish. After this ink has been removed, no matter how completely it can be detected by dipping the paper into a solution of ammonium sulphide.

IV.

Aniline black in crystals	1 part.
Alcohol	30 "
Glycerine	30 "

Dissolve in the alcohol, and add the glycerine afterwards.

Show Card Ink.—

Pure asphaltum	16 parts.
Venice turpentine	18 "
Lamp-black	4 "
Oil of turpentine	64 "

Dissolve the asphaltum in the turpentine, and thoroughly mix.

Stencil Ink.—Shellac, 2 ounces; borax, 2 ounces; water, 25 ounces. Dissolve by heat if necessary, first the borax alone, and then adding the shellac. To the clear solution add gum arabic, 2 ounces. Color with lamp-black, with Venetian red, or with ultramarine, to suit the taste. Another formula gives shellac, 4 parts, borax, 1 part, and omits the gum arabic.

Copying Ink (for use without a press by simply pressing and rubbing with the hand), by Prof. Attfield, F.R.S.—Use ink of any kind of extra strength.

This in many cases can be made by evaporating common ink down to six tenths of its volume. Then mix with it two thirds of its volume of glycerine, so as to restore the original volume.

White Ink.—Barium sulphate, or "flake white" is mixed with gum arabic water of sufficient thickness to keep it suspended, at least while in use. Starch or magnesium carbonate or other white powder may be used instead of the barium sulphate. The powder must be of impalpable fineness.

White Ink on Blue Paper.—A solution of oxalic acid in water is used for this purpose. It may be applied with a rubber stamp or with a common pen. A quill or gold pen is the best as a steel pen is soon corroded. The ink bleaches the paper wherever it touches it, giving white lines on a blue ground.

Gold Ink.—Gold leaf with honey is ground up in a mortar, best an agate mortar, or on a painters' slab with a muller. It is added to water, and thoroughly mixed and at once poured off from the first sediments, filtered out, and washed. This is done to secure the impalpably finely ground gold only. The resulting powder is mixed with a suitable vehicle, such as white varnish or gum arabic water.

Silver Ink.—As above, using silver leaf.

Zinc Label Ink.—I. Verdigris, 1 part; ammonium chloride, 1 part; lamp-black, ¼ part; water, 10 parts.

II. Platinum bichloride, 1 part; gum arabic, 1 part; water, 10 parts.

Diamond Ink for Etching Glass.—This consists essentially of hydrofluoric acid mixed with barium sulphate to the consistency of cream. The barium sulphate is quite inoperative except as giving a body to prevent the ink from spreading. It is applied with a rubber stamp or pen and allowed to remain for ten minutes or until dry. On removal of the white powder, the design will be found etched on the glass. The following is a formula for it.

Saturate hydrofluoric acid with ammonia, add an equal volume of hydrofluoric acid and thicken with barium sulphate in fine powder.

CHAPTER XVIII.

MISCELLANEOUS.

To Soften and Restore India Rubber Hose, etc.—I. Dip in petroleum and hang up for a couple of days. Repeat process if necessary.

II. The above process is applicable to all articles, but is specified for hose. It is stated that old rubber that has become hard may be softened by exposure first to vapor of carbon disulphide, followed by exposure to the vapor of kerosene. The latter vapor is found to be a general preservative for india rubber.

III. Dr. Pol recommends immersion in a solution of water of ammonia, 1 part, and water 2 parts, from a few minutes to an hour.

To Prevent Decay of Rubber Tubing.—The decay of rubber tubing has been attributed to the formation of sulphuric acid from the sulphur mixed with it. M. Ballard has suggested washing with water or weak alkaline solution five or six times in a year.

Joints between India Rubber Tubing and Metal.—Where tubing is temporarily slipped over metal gas pipes and similar connections, as in the chemical laboratory, it is well to apply glycerine to the metal.

It acts as a lubricant in slipping the tubing on, and assists in its withdrawal.

Preserving Vulcanite.—Wash occasionally with a solution of ammonia and rub with a rag slightly moistened with kerosene oil.

Effect of Copper upon Rubber.—In a paper read before the recent meeting of the British Association, Sir William Thomson stated that metallic copper, when heated to the temperature of boiling water, in contact with the rubber, exerted a destructive effect upon it. With a view to finding whether this was due to the copper *per se,* or to its power of conducting heat more rapidly to the rubber, he laid a sheet of rubber on a plate of glass, and on it placed four clean disks, one of copper, one of platinum, one of zinc and one of silver. After a few days in an incubator at 150° F., the rubber under the copper had become quite hard, that under the platinum had become slightly affected and hardened at different parts, while the rubber under the silver and under the zinc was quite hard and elastic. This would warrant the inference that the metallic copper had exerted a great oxidizing effect on the rubber, the platinum had exerted a slight effect, while the zinc and silver respectively had no injurious influence on it. The rubber thus hardened by the copper contained, strange enough, no appreciable trace of copper; the copper, therefore, presumably sets up the oxidizing action in the rubber without itself permeating it.

Gas Tight Tubings.—Fletcher has invented a gas tight rubber tubing in which a layer of tinfoil is interposed between two concentric rubber tubes, all vulcanized together.

Printing Colors upon India Rubber.—It may sometimes be desirable to have a surface of vulcanized india rubber so prepared that it will take colors such as are used for calico printing. This end is simply attained by sprinkling the article with farina before vulcanizing. A small quantity attaches itself and forms an excellent base for color printing.

Gutta-Percha for Coating Glass.—For focusing glass in photography and for similar purposes where ground glass or a translucent material is required, a solution of gutta-percha in chloroform is highly recommended. This is flowed over or painted on the glass and is allowed to evaporate afterwards.

Burned Rubber.—A very soft pure gum sold for artists' use is improperly termed burned rubber. It is used in crayon work for removing and lightening marks by dabbing it against the paper, cleaning the rubber from time to time. It is so soft that it picks up and removes crayon marks without the necessity of friction. Thus the rubbing out or more properly erasing operation can be localized and crayon tints can be lightened in tone without impairment or "smutting." It is a very elegant accessory to the artists' paraphernalia. To make it, pure virgin gum, preferably the best Para, is cut into pieces and soaked for some hours in benzole. A long soaking is advisable. The pieces are then removed from the benzole and are ground in a mortar until perfectly homogeneous. The mass is gathered up with a spatula and is pressed into little tin boxes. If desired it may be dried upon a water bath. This is not necessary as, if the box is left open, it will rapidly season itself. It should be very soft, should tend to adhere to the fingers, yet should leave them easily, and should strip cleanly from the box. A very little turpentine makes it more adhesive. It may even be softened in turpentine alone. This gives a gum that seasons more slowly and is in some respects preferable to the benzole made preparation. It is sold at a high price by the dealers, as the demand for it is limited.

Rubber Sponge.—This is also an artist's rubber. It is also used for cleaning kid gloves. It is made by incorporating with the masticated or washed and sheeted gum any material or materials that will give off vapor in the curing process. Damp sawdust and crystallized alum are used as giving off vapor of water or steam, or ammonium carbonate as giving off vapors of ammonia carbonic acid gas and steam. The mixed gum may be cured in moulds, which it will fill by its expansion.

Shellac Varnish for India Rubber.—This is made by soaking powdered shellac in ten times its weight of strong aqua ammonia (26° B.). At first no change beyond a coloring of the solution is perceptible. After many days standing the bottle, which should have a glass stopper, being tightly closed, the shellac disappears, having entered into solution. It may be a month before complete solution. This forms an excellent varnish for india rubber shoes and similar articles. It may be applied with a rag. It is also a good application for leather in some cases and doubtless many other uses could be made of it. It would act well as a vehicle for a dark pigment such as lamp-black. It will rejuvenate a pair of india rubbers very nicely. The ammonia exercises also a good influence on the rubber. It has been recommended as a cement for attaching rubber to metal, but its adhesive powers are not always satisfactory.

Simple Substitute for Stamps.—A very simple though rough and imperfect substitute may be made by gluing with common carpenter's glue pieces of thick string upon a piece of wood, the string being given the form of the desired letters. Care must be taken to avoid saturating and stiffening the string with the glue.

India Rubber Substitutes.—One of these under the name of vulcanized oil is thus described by Bolas:

"Vulcanized oil is, perhaps, of more interest, and many oils, such as linseed and others resembling it, may be vulcanized by being heated for some time to 150° Centigrade with twelve to twenty per cent. of sulphur. The product obtained is soft, and somewhat resembles very bad india rubber. By increasing the proportion of sulphur very much indeed, say to four times the weight of the oil, and vulcanizing at a higher temperature, a hard substance, resembling inferior vulcanite, is obtained.

"Soft and hard vulcanized oil have been introduced into commerce at various times and under many names; but these materials never seem to have made very much headway."

Another method of treating the oil consists in mixing it with a solution of chloride of sulphur in carbon disulphide or in naptha. On standing, the volatile solvents escape, leaving a thick mass, which is the substitute.

In combinations of aluminum with the fatty acids, forming aluminum soaps, and of these, aluminum palmitate especially, a substitute for india rubber has been sought but without success.

Metallized Caoutchouc.—Unvulcanized gum is mixed with powdered lead, zinc, or antimony. The mixed india rubber is then cured as in the regular process.

EMERY WHEELS AND WHETSTONES.

Bolas thus describes their manufacture:

"When ordinary vulcanized rubber is heated to 230° Centigrade, (446° F.) or until it melts, a permanently viscous product is obtained, and this substance, if mixed with emery and sulphur to a kind of paste, forms a material out of which the so-called agglomerated emery wheels or grinders may be formed, the mixed materials being next hardened or cured by the application of a steam heat. Emery wheels and hones made on this principle were introduced by Deplanque about twenty-three years ago.

"Thirty-five parts of old vulcanized caoutchouc having been placed in a kind of still, heat is applied to melt it, the operation being assisted by the gradual addition of about ten parts of heavy coal oil; but this latter is afterward distilled off. The softened caoutchouc is then incorporated with 500 parts of emery of the required degree of fineness and nine parts of sulphur. These materials having been thoroughly mixed, the hones or wheels are manufactured, and afterward cured or baked at a heat of 140° Centigrade, (284° F.) during a period of about eight hours. Grinding wheels, made in the above manner, can be worked at a speed of 2,000 revolutions per minute, and are extremely useful for the working of hardened steel or other obdurate materials."

Etching on Metals and Glass.—India rubber stamps can be used for placing the ground upon knife blades and similar articles which are to be etched. The parts untouched by the stamp are attacked by the acid. In the case of glass, diamond ink (page 133) can be put on with a stamp. The acids for metal etching might be thickened with barium sulphate also and applied in the same way. In these cases the inscription of the stamp would be etched. Where ground is put on, whether on glass or metal, the design for the stamp will be protected.

Etching Ground for Metals.—Equal parts of asphalt, Burgundy pitch and beeswax melted together and mixed thoroughly. It may be softened with mutton suet. Beeswax may be used, dissolved in ether or simply melted. Yellow soap is sufficient for ordinary work.

Etching Solutions for Biting in.—For steel and iron, *a.* sulphate of copper and common salt in solution. *b.* sulphate of copper, sulphate of alumina, and common salt, of each two drachms; acetic acid, 1½ oz. *c.* sulphuric acid, diluted with five volumes of water with a little sulphate of copper. For other metals, except gold and platinum, nitric acid diluted with five volumes of water.

Etching Ground for Glass.—Melted beeswax is generally recommended. It can be removed with spirits of turpentine after as much as possible has been scraped off.

Etching Glass.—Glass may be conveniently etched by exposing it to the vapor of hydrofluoric acid. A shallow leaden tray, as large as the glass, is required. A quantity of fluorspar is placed in it and is moistened with concentrated sulphuric acid. The glass is placed face downward over the tray. It is supported over the mixture by resting on the edges of the tray or by any simple method, and the whole is covered with a towel. In half an hour or more the etching will be completed. The vapors must not be allowed to escape into any room containing glass or metal articles as they corrode everything. Great care should be taken also not to let the mixture touch the hand, as painful ulcers are the result.

India Rubber Shoe Blacking.—Raw india rubber is given as a constituent of several shoe blackings. Formulæ are given as below for paste and liquid blackings.

I. Paste blacking: bone-black, 20 parts; molasses, 15 parts; vinegar, 4 parts; sulphuric acid, 4 parts; caoutchouc oil (as given below), 3 parts.

II. Liquid blacking: bone-black, 60 parts; molasses, 45 parts; gum arabic dissolved in water, 1 part; vinegar, 50 parts; sulphuric acid, 24 parts; caoutchouc oil, 9 parts.

Caoutchouc oil is made by dissolving or digesting virgin rubber 55 parts in linseed oil 450 parts.

Waterproof Composition for Boots.—One ounce of virgin rubber cut into pieces is digested in enough oil of turpentine to form a stiff paste. In applying heat take great care lest the contents of the vessel become ignited. When homogeneous, which condition may be brought about by rubbing in a porcelain mortar, as described in chapter XII., it is mixed with 5-6 ounces of boiled linseed oil. This gives an ointment almost of the consistency of butter.

INDEX.

	PAGE
ABSORPTION of sulphur process..	100
Absorption of water by india rubber	31
Africa, ways of collecting rubber sap	15-17
Analysis of sap of india rubber tree	27
Apparatus for stamp making	61-63
Artists' burned rubber	136-137
BALLOONS	95
Bands, india rubber	41
Bicycle tyre cement	125
Blacking, india rubber	142
Borax and water solution of rubber	106-107
Brazil, ways of collecting sap	20-21
Bromine as vulcanizer	100
Bulbs, how made	92-93
Burned rubber, artists'	136-137
CALENDERING	43
Cane tips	90
Caoutchin	30
Caoutchoucin	30
Caoutchouc, (see India Rubber.)	
Cements	125-128
Clamp for vulcanizing press	52
Cohesion of rubber, its importance to the manufacturer	26-27
Cold curing	100-102
Composition for stamps and its moulding	113-120
Composition inking pad	118-119
Composition stamp handle	117-118
Cord, rubber	92
Corks	90-91
Curing	44
Curing, how to judge of completion of	70
Curing in liquid bath	97
Curing in sulphur bath	99
Curing, temperature of	58
Central America, ways of collecting rubber	18-19
Chair leg tips	90
Chalk plates	83-84
Chlorine as vulcanizer	100
Chloroform as a solvent	105
Coagulation of sap by a plant	19
Coagulation of sap by alum	22-23
Coagulation of sap by fire	21-22
Coagulation of sap by salt	18
Cohesion of pure rubber	25
DATING stamps, composition	116-117
Didot's polytype for matrices	82-83
Distillation products of india rubber	29-30
Dolls, how made	92-93
EBONITE	108-111
Ebonite, polishing	110-111

144 INDEX.

Emery wheels and whetstones ... 139, 140
Emulsion of caoutchouc 10
Etching 140-142

Fins, removal of 86
Flask for type moulding 74
Flong matrices 80-82
Flong paste 80
Fluid for mixing with plaster for matrices 55

Gas heated steam vulcanizer 53
Glue, marine 126
Glue stamps 113-120
Glycerine bath for curing 97
Goodyear, Charles 13-14
Gutta-percha 111-112
Gutta-percha, moulding 111-112
Gutta-percha, vulcanizing 111

Hektograph, composition 121-122, 124
Hektograph, how made and used 121-124
Hektograph ink (also see inks).. 121
Hektograph sheets 124

India Rubber, absorption of water by 31
India rubber, African 15-17
India rubber, artists' burned 136-137
India rubber, availability for small articles 85
India rubber, cohesion of unvulcanized 25
India rubber, composition of 27
India rubber, discovery of, etc. 11-13
India rubber, effects of temperature on 28-29
India rubber, elasticity of ....
India rubber sap, its coagulation 11

India rubber sheet, how made.. 40
India rubbers, original way of making 10
India rubber stamp making without apparatus 71
India rubber stamps, home-made mould 48-50
India rubber stamps, starting point 47
India rubber, trees producing.. 9
India rubber tree sap, analysis of 27
India rubber type. 73
India rubber, vulcanized, general properties of 32-33
India rubber, where collected, 11
India rubber, inelastic, how made 31
India rubber, its mastication.. 38-40
India rubber, manufacture of, 35-46
India rubber, necessity of drying 38
India rubber, points to be followed in moulding small articles 85
India rubber, preliminary operations in manufacturing 35-36
India rubber, preserving, etc. 134-135
India rubber, properties of 28
India rubber sap 9-11
India rubber stamp vulcanizing 58-60
Inelastic state of india rubber.. 31
Inks, special for stamping, etc. 129-133
Iodine and haloid vulcanizers... 100
Isoprene 30

Leaves, skeletonized as models. 92
Liquid bath curing 97

Machine for cutting sheet and threads 40
Machine for making mixed sheet 42-43

INDEX. 145

Machine for masticating...... 38–40
Machine for washing and sheeting................ 37
Mackintosh.................... 13
Mackintoshes, how made...... 45–46
Marshmallow not for mixture with plaster........... 57
Masticated rubber, its easy solution... 103–104
Masticating in mortar with benzole........ 103–104
Mastication of rubber.........38–40
Materials mixed with india rubber........ 43
Matrices, various kinds of, for stamps................ 80–84
Matrix for stamp-making. .. 54–55
Matrix making by casting..... 56–57
Matrix press......... 56
Matrix, process of making, for stamps............... 54–55
Mats 91–92
Metals, welding and cohesion of 25–26
Miscellaneous 134–142
Mixed sheet................. 42–44
Mixed sheet for stamps....... 47–48
Mould, home-made for stamps. 48–50
Moulding and curing stamps.. 58–60
Moulds for composition stamps, temperature of 120
Moulds, material for............ 86

Naptha and volatile solvents, danger of.................... 107
Naptha, solvent............. 104–105
Nicaragua, ways of collecting sap.... 19–20
Nitric acid as vulcanizer........ 100

Oil for composition stamp moulds 119–120

Oil for mould face.............. 55
Oils fixed bad effect on solutions..................... 105
Oxychloride of zinc cement for matrices...................... 57

Papier maché matrices....... 80–82
Paraffin and rubber. 105–106
Parkes' process..............100–102
Payen's solvent....... 105
Pencil tips, moulds for....... 89–90
Phenyle sulphide as softener of vulcanized rubber............ 106
Plaster dental for matrices.. ... 54
Press for moulding stamps, etc. 51–52
Press, gas-heated............. 52–53
Press, home-made 49
Press, matrix making.......... 55–56
Products, general division of.. 35–36

Rods, stirring for laboratory... 95
Rubber, origin of name.... 12
Rubber, see India Rubber......

Salt bath for curing.......... 98
Sap of india rubber tree, analysis of........................... 27
Sheeting and washing....... 37–38
Sheet rubber, how made... 40
Sheet rubber, its joining........ 94
Shellac for strengthening matrix
Shoes, blacking for............. 142
Shoes, india rubber, cement for. 127
Siphonia, origin of name......... 11
Solution, different views of... 31–32
Solution, difficulties of.......... 103
Solvents for rubber......... 104–105
Spring chase for matrices....... 56
Springs for stamp moulds...... 51
Springs on moulding press... ,. 51
Sponge india rubber........... 137
Stamp making.... 47

Stamps, rubber, substitute for. 138
Stamps, see India Rubber, Composition and general titles.
Strauss' method of coagulating sap 22-23
Suction discs, regular mould for 88-89
Suction discs, simple mould for 87-88
Sulphides, alkaline as vulcanizers.................... 100
Sulphur, absorption process.... 100
Sulphur bath for mixing and curing.................... 98-100
Sulphur chloride process.... 100-102
Sulphur, how mixed with gum.. 43
Sulphur, its escape from vulcanized rubber.................... 33-34
Sunlight excluded from washed sheet rubber.................... 38
Syringes made by Indians...... 11

Test for curing with knife...... 48
Thread, rubber, cut............ 41
Thread, rubber, moulded....... 92
Tissues, coated, how made.... 45-46
Tubes, connecting glass........ 96
Tube, seamless................. 92
Turpentine, a solvent for vulcanized rubber. 106
Turpentine compared with caoutchoucin.................... 30
Turpentine, viscid nature of solution.................... 104-105
Type, india rubber............. 73

Type moulding flask.... 74
Type and stamps from vulcanized rubber.................... 77
Type, cutting apart 75
Type, points in moulding....... 75
Type, quads, and spaces for stamp models.................... 71-72
Type, steel moulds for.......... 76

United States composition stamps.................... 113-120

Varnish shellac for india rubber.................... 137-138
Vulcanite...... 108-111
Vulcanization, its two steps..... 42
Vulcanization, steps in process.................... 47-48
Vulcanized rubber stamps and type.................... 77
Vulcanizer.................... 52-53
Vulcanizer, fish kettle as a... 69-70
Vulcanizer, flower pot.. 68-70
Vulcanizer, chamber............ 63
Vulcanizing and moulding stamps.................... 58-60

Washing and sheeting....... 37-38
Water absorbed by india rubber. 31
Waterproof composition for shoes 142
Waterproofing for battery cells.................... 127-128

Zinc, chloride.................... 57

ARITHMETIC
OF
ELECTRICITY

By T. O'Conor Sloane, A.M., E.M., Ph.D.

THIS work gives the practical Electric Calculations in such a simple manner that they can be used by any one having a knowledge of Arithmetic. It treats of calculations for wiring; resistance in general; arrangement of batteries for different work, heating effects of currents, calculations of size of fusible safety catches, electro-plating calculations, voltage of untried combinations, and distribution of work in compound circuits, and all other practical calculations of heat, work and energy; and is supplemented by the most practical series of tables ever published. In a separate chapter the deductions of the rules are given. Each rule after statement and explanation is followed by one or more fully worked out practical examples. It makes Electrical Calculations intelligible to all, and may justly be said to fill a new field. It is absolutely indispensable to the working electrician, as well as to the professor, scientific teacher, student and amateur.

Fully Illustrated. Price, $1.00.

NORMAN W. HENLEY & CO.

P. O. Box 3271,

150 NASSAU STREET,   NEW YORK.

GEO. R. BLAKELY,

Manufacturer of

❋—BANKING AND COMMERCIAL—❋

RUBBER ❋ STAMPS

❋ STENCILS, SEAL PRESSES, WAX SEALS, ❋
❋ BURNING BRANDS, DOOR PLATES AND ❋
❋ HOUSE NUMBERS, BAGGAGE AND ❋
❋ KEY CHECKS, SOLID AND METAL- ❋
❋ BODIED RUBBER TYPE, SOLID ❋
❋ RUBBER DATES, NUMBER- ❋
❋ ING MACHINES, DATING ❋
❋ STAMPS OF ALL KINDS, ❋
❋ CLOTHING STENCILS, PRINTING ❋
❋ WHEELS, ETC. ❋

IF IN NEED OF ANY OF THE ABOVE, PLEASE WRITE FOR SAMPLES AND PRICES.

BRADFORD, McKEAN CO., PA.

PRACTICAL TRADE MANUALS.

Copley's Plain and Ornamental Alphabets.—Examples in every style, Mechanical and Analytical Construction of Letters. Designs for Titles, Ciphers, Monograms, Borders, Compasses, Flourishes, etc. *New Edition.* Price..................................$2.00

Book of Alphabets.—For Painters, Draughtsmen, Designers, etc. All standard styles and many new and popular ones, German, French, Old English, etc. Price........ .... 50 cts.

Album of Fancy Alphabets.—For Sign Painters. It gives the fashionable styles of the day. Price................,.......... 75 cts.

Sign, Carriage and Decorative Painting.—Full of valuable points upon the several branches of the trade. It includes Fresco and Car Painting, and other useful matters. Price ... .50 cts.

Landa's Fancy Alphabets.—These alphabets are the production of a French artist and have long been favorites with draughtsmen and others in America. Cloth.. ....$1.00

Standard Scroll Book, The.—A collection of upward of two hundred designs, for painters, jewelers, designers, decorators, and every branch requiring ornamental scroll work. It must be seen to be appreciated. Prominent features in this book are the shaded scrolls, and the designs for signs, wagons and omnibuses. Price $1.00

How to Draw and Paint.—The whole art of Drawing and Painting, containing concise instructions in outline, light and shade, perspective, sketching from nature, etc., etc. One hundred illustrations. Boards, cloth back. Price.... .... 50 cts.

Gilder's Manual.—A guide to gilding in all its branches as used in the several trades, such as interior decoration, picture and looking-glass frames, oil and water gilding, regilding, gilding china, glass, china, pottery, etc., etc. Price.................................. ..50 cts.

The Standard Sign Writer.—The Standard work on the subject. Its instructions are clear, precise, and practical, and cover just the ground desired by most of the profession. Price.......$2.00

1000 Specimens of Monograms, adapted to the use of Painters, Printers, Engravers, Stamp Makers, Stamping and General Designing. Paper cover........ ....50 cts.

Use of Colors.—Valuable treatise on the properties of different pigments and their suitableness to uses of artists and students. Price ....25 cts.

Scene Painting and Painting in Distemper.—Gives full instructions in the preparation of the colors, drawing for scene painters, stage settings and useful information regarding stage appliances and effects. Numerous illustrative diagrams and engravings. Price $1.00

Painter's Manual.—A practical guide to house and sign painting, graining, varnishing, polishing, kalsomining, papering, lettering, staining, gilding, glazing, silvering, etc., etc. Including treatise on How to Mix Paints. To the learner the book is simply indispensable. Price... 50 cts.

Sign Writing and Glass Embossing.—A Standard work widely and favorably known; new edition, with newly engraved illustrations and at a greatly reduced price....................75 cts.

Any of the above books sent, post-paid, on receipt of price.

NORMAN W. HENLEY & CO.
P. O. Box 3271,

150 Nassau Street,   NEW YORK.

RUBBER STAMP
MANUFACTURERS' OUTFITS
AND ALL MATERIALS.

VULCANIZERS,

RUBBER,

INKS,

HANDLES,

MOULDING

COMPOUND

SELF-INKING

STAMPS.

POCKET

STAMPS,

SELF-INKING

PADS.

MOULDING

PRESSES,

PEN & PENCIL

STAMPS,

AND EVERY

REQUIREMENT

FOR THE

MANUFAC-

TURE OF RUB-

BER STAMPS.

SEND FOR

A CATALOGUE.

AND MANUFACTURERS OF THE FOLLOWING SPECIALTIES:

Steel Type for Type Writers, Steel Letters and Figures for the Hardware Trade, Brass and Iron Dies for Printing on Wood, Stencil Plates of every Description, Burning Brands, Seals of all kinds, Rubber and Metal Stamps.

NUMBERING MACHINES, CHECK PROTECTORS, BAGGAGE CHECKS, KEY CHECKS, STEEL STAMPS, BRASS LABELS, RIBBON STAMPS, STEEL TYPE, BRASS TYPE, STENCIL DIES, STEEL DIES, STENCIL BRUSHES, INKS AND MATERIALS, REVOLVING STEEL STAMPING FIGURE WHEELS, RAILROAD SEALS, RUBBER TYPE, SOAP DIES AND STAMPS.

DIE SINKERS AND GENERAL ENGRAVERS.

NEW YORK STENCIL WORKS,
P. O. BOX 3581.

Telephone Call 1340 Cortlandt.
Cable Address, Proplastic, New York.

100 Nassau Street, New York.

Facts Worth Knowing.

For the Household, Workshop, and Farm. Edited by T. O'Conor Sloane, A. M., E. M., Ph.D. 250 Illustrations.

This large and fully illustrated volume is made up of selections from the Scientific American. It covers a wide territory, natural science, home work, household receipts, health, the farm, and all other topics are treated in characistic articles in its 878 pages. Price, $3.50.

Home Experiments in Science.

For Old and Young, a repertory of simple experiments with home-made apparatus, by T. O'Conor Sloane, A.M., E.M., Ph.D. 97 Illustrations.

This beautifully illustrated work treats of experiments in physics, and is addressed to all scientific teachers, students and amateurs. It is really a succinct manual of physics, with simple experiments to illustrate its teachings. Price, $1.50.

NORMAN W. HENLEY & CO.
P. O. Box 3271,
150 Nassau Street,   **NEW YORK.**

A HANDY COMPANION.

PAYNE'S BUSINESS POINTERS.

Containing much information necessary to success in business comprising *New Tariff complete; Passport Regulations; Rates of Foreign Postage; Naturalization Laws; How to Indorse Checks;* Debt of U. S.; Wages Table; Official Titles—Military, Scholastic, Naval, and Professional; Educational Statistics of the World; *Business Laws; Legal Forms used in Business,* such as Power of Attorney, Notes, Drafts, Leases, Receipts, Protests, Bills of Lading, Private Marks of Prices, and many other forms; *Dictionary of Mercantile Terms;* How to Measure Land; *Legal Rates of Interest; Rates of Postage in U. S.;* new American Value of Foreign Gold and Silver Coins; 1,899 Interesting Facts; Interest Laws of U. S.; Copyright Law; Interest Tables—5, 6, 7, 8, and 10 per cent; Population of United States, 1890; Table of Weights and Measures and the Metric System; List of Abbreviations used in business; Latin, French, Spanish, and Italian Words and Phrases; Marks and Rules of Punctuation and Accent; Use of Capital Letters; *Complete Dictionary of Synonyms,* etc., etc., making in all the most complete and cheapest Business Encyclopedia ever issued. 212 pages, bound in extra paper cover, *price 25 cents; extra cloth 50 cents.*

For sale by all booksellers, or sent post-paid on receipt of price.

INVENTOR'S MANUAL

How to Make a Patent Pay

BY AN EXPERIENCED AND SUCCESSFUL INVENTOR.

Thousands of useful inventions are every year patented, but on which the inventor does not realize anything, simply for want of information how best to proceed to introduce or dispose of his invention.

The INVENTOR'S MANUAL is a book designed as a guide to inventors in perfecting their inventions, taking out their patents, and disposing of them. It is not in any sense a Patent Solicitor's Circular, nor a Patent Broker's Advertisement. No advertisements of any description appear in the work. It is a book of about 100 pages, containing a quarter of a century's experience of a successful inventor, together with notes based upon the experience of many other inventors.

CLOTH, PRICE, POST-PAID, $1.00.

NORMAN W. HENLEY & CO.

P. O. Box 3271.   150 NASSAU STREET,

NEW YORK.

SPANGENBERG'S

Quick Process

Moulding Press and Vulcanizer.

* * *

IS undoubtedly the Best Machine of its kind ever introduced.

* * *

* * *

STRONG, Compact, Durable. It is no Toy but a complete practical Rubber Stamp Machine.

* * *

If you want to make Rubber Stamps Quick and Easy, and do it along with your regular business, or in leisure hours,

THIS IS JUST THE THING YOU WANT

Price, complete, with 5 lbs. Moulding Composition and 1 lb. Rubber, $20.00.

L. SPANGENBERG,

194 Broadway, - - New York.

STAFFORD'S STENCIL COMBINATIONS

ARE USEFUL FOR MANY PURPOSES.

Each Combination consists of the Alphabet from A to &, Figures 1 to 0, Stencil Ink and Brush.

Eight Sizes are made, viz., ½, ¾, 1, 1¼, 1½, 1¾, 2, 2½ inches.

PRICE LIST.

Size, inches,	½	¾	1	1¼	1½	1¾	2	2½
Per dozen,	$9.60	10.80	10.80	15.00	16.80	19.80	19.80	30.00

Liberal Discount to the Trade.

STENCIL AND RUBBER STAMP SUPPLIES, METAL BADGES AND CHECKS.

---SEND FOR CATALOGUE---

ARTHUR STAFFORD,
35 and 37 Beekman Street, New York.

JUST PUBLISHED

HINTS TO POWER USERS

PLAIN, PRACTICAL POINTERS, FREE FROM HIGH SCIENCE, AND INTENDED FOR THE MAN WHO PAYS THE BILLS

BY

Robert Grimshaw, M. E., Etc.

Author of "Steam Engine Catechism," "Pump Catechism," "Boiler Catechism," "Preparing for Indication," "Engineers' Hourly Log Book," and other Practical Books.

1 Vol. 16mo, Cloth. Price, $1.00.

Under the above title the well-known engineering expert, Mr. Robert Grimshaw, whose catechisms of the Steam Engine, Pump and Boiler, and other practical works, have proved so popular among working engineers, has prepared some meaty non-technical advice to the men who pay the bills. Having proved his ability to put expert engineering knowledge into a style suitable to interest and instruct the men who run engines, pumps and boilers of every description, he has gone further, and prepared for those having no practical knowledge whatever of steam engineering, good sound advice, in good plain English, as to what to do and what not to do in choosing, buying, placing, and operating every part of a power plant. From ash-pit to exhaust-head, from fly-wheel to belt-lace, no item seems to escape him.

NORMAN W. HENLEY & CO.

P. O. Box 3271,

150 Nassau Street,   NEW YORK.

www.ingramcontent.com/pod-product-compliance
Lightning Source LLC
Chambersburg PA
CBHW030317170426
43202CB00009B/1040